Leveraging Data for Student Success: Improving Education Through Data-Driven Decisions

Laura G. Knapp, Elizabeth Glennie,
and Karen J. Charles

RTI Press

The RTI Press mission is to disseminate information about RTI research, analytic tools, and technical expertise to a national and international audience. RTI Press publications are peer-reviewed by at least two independent substantive experts and one or more Press editors.

RTI International is an independent, nonprofit research organization dedicated to improving the human condition by turning knowledge into practice. RTI offers innovative research and technical services to governments and businesses worldwide in the areas of health and pharmaceuticals, education and training, surveys and statistics, advanced technology, international development, economic and social policy, energy and the environment, and laboratory testing and chemistry services.

Library of Congress Control Number: 2016954669

ISBN 978-1-934831-20-5
(refers to print version)

RTI Press publication No. BK-0018-1609
http://dx.doi.org/10.3768/rtipress.2016.bk.0018.1609
www.rti.org/rtipress

Cover design: Danielle Hennis

This publication is part of the RTI Press Book series.

RTI International
3040 East Cornwallis Road, PO Box 12194
Research Triangle Park, NC 27709-2194, USA
rtipress@rti.org
www.rti.org

Contents

Acknowledgments v

Introduction vii

1. Planning to Make Data-Driven Decisions 1
Introduction 1
Defining College Readiness 2
Using Data to Solve Problems and Answer Questions: An Example 5
Using Logic Models as Planning and Evaluation Tools 10
Developing a Comprehensive Analysis Plan 15

2. Obtaining Data 23
Introduction 23
Collecting Student Data 24
Accessing State and District Data Systems 28
Accessing Postsecondary Data 36
Effective Methods for Collecting Data 39
Protecting the Privacy and Security of Student Data 46

3. Measuring and Managing Data 55
Introduction 55
Defining and Measuring Variables 56
Converting Concepts to Variables 57
Data Quality 62
Merging Data Files 67
Documenting the Process 76

4. Data Analysis 81
Introduction 81
Choosing Appropriate Analysis Techniques 82
Strategies for Selecting Comparison Groups 83
Choosing an Analytic Technique 86

5. Dissemination 95
Introduction 95
Understanding and Supporting Your Audience 97
Disseminating Findings through Various Media 102

(continued)

References   107

Additional Resources   111

Glossary   113

Contributors   121

Tables

1. Applying the scientific method in the classroom and beyond   5

2. Longitudinal dataset tracking students' progress through middle school   29

3. Number of states adopting new Data Quality Campaign actions   32

4. States taking additional steps to develop statewide longitudinal data systems (SLDSs)   33

5. Sample multiple-choice survey questions   41

6. Examples of the process of defining variables   59

7. Data merge results from two different student records   72

8. Data collection codebook sample entries   77

9. Sample data tracking table   78

10. Disseminating dual-enrollment information to students and parents   99

11. Disseminating dual-enrollment information to administrators   99

12. Disseminating dual-enrollment information to funders and policy makers 100

13. Disseminating dual-enrollment information to program staff   101

14. Use of information comparisons: hypothetical versus actual   101

15. Common dissemination strategies   102

Figures

1. Logic model for selecting a postsecondary school   12

2. Logic model for developing a new high school math class   13

3. Sample mobile device survey question   42

4. Sample online rating scale survey question   43

5. Example of text-to-table relationship   105

Acknowledgments

Funding for this work was provided by RTI International and US Department of Education contract ED-PEP-11-C-0059. Authors are grateful for that support and for the assistance and thoughtful comments of Barbara Elliott, Ruth Heuer, Marcinda Mason and Chrissy Tillery.

Introduction

How effective is your educational program? Is your program working the way you intended? Are students responding to services in the way you hoped? Can you attribute student outcomes to your program?

Educators ask these kinds of questions when considering whether to continue, expand, or modify services. You may want to expand services that work well and adjust those that need improvement. If an innovative strategy benefits students, you might want to share that information with other educational service providers so that they can build on that strategy. You may be required to provide a final report to the organization that funds your program to demonstrate the program's success.

Data can be collected and analyzed to address these questions. Data-driven decision making means using a logical, evidence-based approach to actions.

Different kinds of educators regularly make data-driven decisions as part of their job. Project directors collect and review data to report on the status of the project and initiate changes if the data reveal that the project is missing its targets. Principals engage their teachers in collecting and reviewing data to inform the school's continuous improvement plan. District superintendents review school data to make decisions about allocating new services. Classroom teachers use data as part of their instructional practices. They may not credit themselves with using data to monitor student learning, but they gauge every question, probe, and student response to understand students' levels of understanding.

What kinds of data should be collected and analyzed to address various educational questions? Advances in database technology allow educators to collect vast amounts of student data, but not all of it is relevant to teaching and learning. You need to decide which items to use. You may have enough data to address your questions, but you may need to put it together in a way that permits addressing your questions. You may need to collect additional information to understand the influence of your program more completely. You need to understand strategies for analyzing the data.

The purpose of this book is to build the capacity of educators at all levels—state and district officials, school administrators, project directors, and classroom teachers—to gather, analyze, and use data to improve the day-to-day learning experiences for students. It is intended to be informal, taking the reader through the typical steps of planning a study that can be as informal as a tally or as formal as an experimental evaluation. Different questions require different approaches, and you can use many strategies to assess the effectiveness of new ideas, approaches, and activities. Chapter 1 describes key steps in planning any study that involves the use of data—identifying the problem, developing evaluation tools, and defining evaluation terms and the related metrics for measuring outcomes. Chapter 2 presents approaches for obtaining and collecting student-level data, and Chapter 3 highlights strategies for measuring variables, managing data, and creating files for analysis. Chapter 4 describes analysis techniques to address different kinds of questions, and Chapter 5 shares guidelines for dissemination. We conclude the book by providing a list of references, a compendium of additional resources, and a glossary of terms for you to refer to throughout.

CHAPTER 1

Planning to Make Data-Driven Decisions

Introduction

Whether you serve in a school, district, or state leadership role, at some point you will be asked to address a prevalent challenge (e.g., lower graduation rates), justify a recent program decision (e.g., implementing dual-enrollment courses), or examine student data (e.g., standardized test scores) to revise existing practices or recommend new approaches. If your program is supported by funding from foundations or grants from the federal government, you may pursue similar questions. Regardless of your role, you have to make decisions that could be more effective with analysis of appropriate data. You need to develop an effective plan, often called a study, for collecting and analyzing data. If your study has any policy implications—and most do—then you want to clearly lay out a plan that confirms you know where you are going, what you are studying, and how the results can be used. Putting time into planning your study defines its boundaries, keeps you focused, and supports implementation as your study moves forward and decisions are made.

This chapter describes key steps in planning any study that involves the use of data—identifying the problem, developing study tools, and defining study terms and the related metrics for measuring the terms. For illustration and consistency, the examples focus on supporting college and career readiness program improvement; however, you are encouraged to investigate the application of this process to studies of other issues that include data collection or analysis.

Identifying a problem or a question represents the starting point for planning a study. Defining the problem is a subtle next step that helps set the boundaries for the study. For example, an identified problem could be that your high school has low graduation rates. By defining the study to include only high school grades, you eliminate any data collection or analysis of middle school metrics. Once defined, your study planning can begin and you can determine if you have enough information to support the study. Studies have specific steps and traditional elements that, when adhered to, contribute to the successful implementation of the study and, ultimately, its credibility.

Logic models and analysis plans are commonly used when designing a study. Logic models help developers organize their thoughts and maintain focus during the planning process. An analysis plan is a roadmap for how you are going to answer your questions. You can revisit and revise these tools during the implementation of the study to support decision making.

Studies require clear definitions, and you should define key terms in the early planning stages. For example, problems in studying college and career readiness programs sometimes relate to the definitions of qualitative attributes such as "college readiness," "career readiness," and being "on track." The metrics used to measure these attributes vary greatly across studies and can lead to results that cannot be compared across projects and programs. When planning your study, defining your terms and the metrics used for quantification are two of the most important elements.

We invite you to explore the ideas in this chapter and use them to your advantage, keeping in mind that studies do not have to be elaborate to be credible. They only need to be planned and executed well. Although this publication is designed for all educators and educational researchers, we primarily focus our examples on college and career readiness. We begin with an explanation of college readiness and then cover other topics that will be expanded in the rest of the book.

Defining College Readiness

College-ready high school students have the knowledge, skills, and characteristics that will allow them to succeed in postsecondary coursework without the need for remediation. Unfortunately, more than one-third of US undergraduates take at least one remedial course in college (Attewell et al., 2006; National Center for Education Statistics, 2011). Further, remedial coursework is a leading indicator that a student will not complete a college degree. However, the need for college remediation is a function of secondary school academic performance and preparation, implying that poor high school preparation is a key factor in reducing students' chances of graduating from college.

Dimensions of College Readiness

There is often a disconnect between what state standards say high school students should learn and what postsecondary institutions expect of high school graduates (Achieve, Inc., 2009). When trying to define or measure college readiness, you want to know the specific content knowledge that should be taught in high school courses for students to enroll and succeed in postsecondary education without the need for remedial classes. To truly be college ready, high school students need to have cognitive strategies such as problem solving, analysis, interpretation, and reasoning; academic knowledge and skills associated with college success, such as writing, synthesis, numeric skills, and research; self-management skills including study skills, time management, and persistence; and knowledge about postsecondary education, such as how to apply to college, how to manage financial aid issues, and how to adjust to college life.

Cognitive Strategies

Conley (2008) identifies cognitive strategies related to college success, including the ability to formulate, investigate, and propose solutions to nonroutine problems; understand and analyze conflicting explanations of phenomena or events; evaluate the credibility and utility of source material and appropriately integrate those sources into a paper or project; think analytically and logically, comparing and contrasting differing philosophies, methods, and positions to understand an issue or concept; and exercise precision and accuracy in applying methods and developing products.

These strategies are at the heart of how postsecondary educators think about their subject areas and what they expect from their students. Students without the capability to think in these ways will struggle as they enter college.

Academic Knowledge and Skills

College writing requires students to present arguments clearly, substantiate each point, and utilize the basics of a style manual when constructing a paper. In addition to writing, college courses increasingly require students to conduct research using appropriate strategies and methodologies to explore and address a range of questions and ideas. In addition to these two overarching academic skills, students need to be well versed in the core academic subjects of English, math, science, social studies, world languages, and the arts.

Self-Management Skills

College students need to keep track of huge amounts of information and organize themselves to meet competing deadlines and priorities. They must plan their time carefully to complete these tasks. They must be able to study independently and in informal and formal study groups. They must know when to seek help from faculty and academic support services and when to cut their losses by dropping a course. These tasks require self-management, a skill that individuals must develop over time, with considerable practice and trial and error.

Knowledge about Postsecondary Education

Comparing colleges, selecting and applying to a postsecondary school, securing financial aid, and adjusting to college life require a tremendous amount of specialized knowledge, including the ability to match personal interests with college majors and programs; understand federal and individual college financial aid programs and how and when to complete the necessary forms; register for, prepare for, and take required admissions exams; apply to college on time and submit all necessary information; and understand how the culture of college is different from that of high school.

Summary

Programs that aid college access often provide a comprehensive set of services that help students prepare to enroll and succeed in postsecondary education. Many of these services are aimed at creating a college-going culture that results in more students who go to college, persist, and graduate. Including services that promote the cognitive strategies and self-management skills can enhance the preparation of students for the rigors of college.

As a potential predictor of college success, remedial college course taking can be used as a proxy for gauging college readiness. The drawback is that you need postsecondary data on your high school graduates, and you may not have the funding to follow them after high school. The advantage is that you may be able to determine which services that you provided to students are associated with lower rates of remedial coursework in college.

If students who participated in a particular service (or group of services) have lower rates of enrollment in remedial courses, then that service(s) may contribute positively to a student's college readiness. However, if students who participated in a service (or group of services) have high rates of enrollment in remedial courses, then that service may not be sufficiently preparing students for college. This information is directly related to the logic model you developed at the outset of your program.

Using Data to Solve Problems and Answer Questions: An Example

Educators have a well-established foundation for solving problems and answering questions. The problems you encounter and the subsequent studies you plan follow much of the process you learned in school as the scientific method. You recognize that you have a problem to solve, gather background information, hypothesize solutions, design a plan to test the solutions, gather and analyze data, draw conclusions, and make recommendations. Regardless of the labels for the various steps you use, you are employing some variation— whether classic or updated—of the scientific method. In general, the researcher devises a plan (design an experiment) that is objective, minimizes bias, manipulates only one variable, and is replicable.

Table 1 shows an example of the scientific method applied to a school science project and an education challenge.

Table 1. Applying the scientific method in the classroom and beyond

Scientific method step	Classroom science (experiment): better burgers	District data (study): remedial math
Purpose: State the Problem	Two fast-food chains both claim to have the tastiest burger.	A high school with high graduation rates does not understand why its graduates have high enrollment rates in remedial math courses at the postsecondary level.
Research: Gather Information	Check websites and other sources to determine the features and composition of both burgers.	Examine freshman enrollment data at postsecondary institutions and corresponding high school transcript data.
Hypothesis: Predict an Outcome	More tasters will choose the burger with the higher fat content.	Students who take a college preparatory math class their senior year in high school will avoid enrollment in remedial math at the postsecondary level.
Design: Prepare the Test	Buy 50 of each burger, enlist classmates to taste and choose.	Develop and implement proposed math class.
Analysis: Examine the Data	Record the choices of the 50 tasters and tally the results.	Gather postsecondary enrollment data on students who did and who did not take the math class.
Conclusion Compare the Findings	Announce whether the hypothesis was proven.	Continue to offer the course if the hypothesis is confirmed.

The steps presented in Table 1 are simplified versions of what really happens and they provide a starting point for exploring how to plan a study. Researchers admit that most models—whether the scientific method, the engineering design process, or some other planning procedure—are guides more than rules and can be adapted or adjusted at most points from start to finish. For ease of discussion here, however, the steps are examined in a logical sequence.

Purpose/State the Problem

Problems, dilemmas, or questions are the genesis for most projects, programs, and studies. Most surface through observation and help define the purpose of the study. Problems may be relatively minor in scope (which laundry detergent best cleans grass stains) or quite important in impact (can a new drug diminish Parkinson's symptoms). You have to ask yourself how you could test various laundry detergents on grass stains or how a drug company could test its new Parkinson's treatment. Good questions are not always easy to formulate because they need to be framed in a way that you can test them.

> **Better burgers.** In the battle of the burgers, even young students realize that both claims that each burger is the "tastiest" cannot be true. For them, the problem becomes "which claim to believe" and how to make that decision about which burger to buy.

> **Remedial math.** A high school diploma should indicate that a student has graduated with proficiency in core academic subjects and is college and career ready. However, a postsecondary math remediation problem persists, especially for minority and first-generation college students.

Research/Gather Information

Gathering background information helps you understand the nature of the problem. It is useful to know whether others have studied the problem, what conjectures others have made, and what evidence supports what theory.

> **Better burger.** Students may decide to investigate the composition of each company's burgers—type of beef, fat content, and other specific ingredients. They might research the sense of taste in an effort to understand taste preferences. They might also try to find the evidence on which each company bases its claim.

Remedial math. School leaders may choose to gather historical data on remedial course enrollment in postsecondary institutions. They might focus on specific student subgroups and review demographic and socioeconomic data, looking for clues that link to school performance. If longitudinal state data on postsecondary remedial math enrollment and students' high school transcripts are available, they might look for course-taking patterns that provide insights.

Hypothesis/Predict an Outcome

Once you identify a problem and review available research, you can formulate an idea—conjecture or hypothesis—to test. You should structure the idea as a statement to be proved or disproved and base it on ideas formulated while building a knowledge base from the research.

Better burger. Suppose that students find out that one burger has a higher fat content than the other, and, at the same time, they discover that fat is pretty tasty. They might develop this hypothesis: *Participants in the study will pick the burger with the higher fat content more often.* In this hypothesis, the students are suggesting a correlation between the fat content and taste based on their understanding of the research conducted.

Remedial math. School leaders are concerned about the math abilities of their graduates who are entering postsecondary institutions. Their data lead them to consider adding a new math course to the local high school curriculum and encouraging college-bound seniors with lower math scores who have not taken advanced methods courses to enroll in the new course. They plan to target seniors who do not plan to take a fourth year of math. Their hypothesis might be: *Low-performing math students who take a college-preparatory math class their senior year in high school are more likely to avoid remedial math classes in college than those who do not.* In this hypothesis, school leaders are proposing an alternate math option for students not taking advanced courses such as calculus or statistics.

Design/Prepare the Test

The core elements of setting up your plan occur here and require attention to detail. A poor design can negate the results of your study. In the study design, you determine who or what is participating and how you selected them, what the variables are, and how you plan to administer the treatment. At this point, you need to understand words such as treatment, control, variables, random, bias, and replication, all of which are in this book's glossary.

The goal is to design a way to test your hypothesis such that you avoid skewing your results to favor one outcome (**bias**) and ensure others can duplicate your procedure. You could introduce bias into the better burger test by using freshly prepared, warm burgers from vendor A and stale, cold burgers from vendor B. You can control for other variables like seasoning and condiments to make sure that the burger meat is the only difference.

Not all studies require the have/have not configuration of treatment and control. In some cases, comparison is achieved in other ways. For the math class, you are not randomly selecting the students for the class (the treatment), but you could compare their results to eligible students who did not enroll in the course. This is still not a true control group as motivation cannot be accounted for, but it can give you satisfactory data for comparison. (Chapter 4 presents information about strategies for developing comparison groups.)

There are additional important topics that are part of the design decisions for a study. These include how many participants (or hamburgers) and how to control for only one variable. The examples below give two illustrations of the study design process.

Better burger. The burger battle has all of the elements required of a good design, but the elements are addressed with modification. Students might describe their design as follows:

1. Get 50 burgers from store A and 50 from store B. Label each one A or B (the variables).

2. Have them prepared identically with the same condiments (control).

3. Enlist 50 volunteer tasters (not a random selection).

4. Give each taster one A and one B (burgers are randomly assigned) and a score card.

5. Ask tasters to record their choice for tastiest burger (no definition of tasty provided).

In this example, it does not make sense to have a control group that tastes no burgers. Instead, your control is that each taster tastes both burgers and chooses one. This approach makes more sense than having half the tasters eat A and half eat B because it ensures that everyone tries both.

Remedial math. The example appears simple at first.

1. Design the new math course.

2. Encourage eligible seniors to take the course (not a random selection).

3. Obtain college course enrollment data on students who took the course (A) and those who did not take the course (B).

4. Determine rates of remedial math enrollment for groups A and B.

This design illustrates one major flaw, and it is one that arises repeatedly when trying to design an experiment with students. Groups A and B are not similar for several reasons. Students in group A may be more motivated, students in group B may have had scheduling conflicts that excluded them from taking the class, and students in each group may have had varying degrees of success in previous math classes. In cases like this, study planners do their best to minimize bias, include an acceptable number of subjects, and design a treatment that is measurable. An alternative is to measure other variables that may influence postsecondary remedial math enrollment and can be controlled in the analysis.

Analysis/Examine the Data

Once the data are collected, you should be able to determine what the results indicate. The type of analysis you choose can be as simple as tallying results, as in voting, or as sophisticated as computer statistical programs allow.

Better burger. In the burger battle, the data are simple and straightforward. Fifty tasters ate both burgers, A and B, and designated their preference. Students in charge of the project tally the responses.

Remedial math. The data are fairly simple in this study as well. Project leaders will collect the enrollment data in postsecondary remedial math courses for the students in their district who did and did not take the special math course in their senior year. They may choose to analyze results to determine the statistical significance of their findings.

Conclusion/Compare the Findings

Conclusions are tricky in that study managers tend to want to generalize beyond the scope of the study. Students may think that they have proven that *all* burgers with high fat content taste better when they have just compared two burger recipes. The remedial math researchers may want to recommend a senior math class to all students based on their findings. However, these researchers do not know whether all students would benefit from this program. In both cases, the researchers need to list the limitations to their study, its design, and the findings.

> **Better burger.** If more students chose the burger with the higher fat content, then the hypothesis is correct. Students will most likely conclude that fat content is a contributor to taste in a burger.

> **Remedial math.** The caution in this study as presented is that several external variables are unaccounted for in the design—student grades, student motivation, former teachers, home influences, outside tutoring, and more. If you find that students who took the extra math class their senior year did avoid remedial postsecondary math courses at a higher rate than students who did not, you can claim a possible link but not an absolute one.

Modifications for Education

The general ideas in these examples lay the foundation for the more specific education applications discussed in the rest of this chapter. You will learn how to plan a study, develop a logic model, and encounter a specific problem (college and career readiness, the default example used throughout).

Using Logic Models as Planning and Evaluation Tools

In its simplest form, a logic model is a visual representation of a series of "if–then" statements that begins with a problem and ends with an array of measurable outcomes. Logic models have been around since the 1970s in the guise of terms such as "theory of change," "hierarchy of evidence" (Bennett, 1975), and "evaluability techniques" (Wholey, 1987). Logic models shift attention from activities to results and, as such, are valuable tools not only for evaluators but for program planners. They are useful as tools of persuasion when presenting an idea to potential funders or relevant stakeholders. As defined by the Kellogg Foundation (2004 p. 1),

A program logic model is a picture of how your program works—the theory and assumptions underlying the program.... This model provides a road map of your program, highlighting how it is expected to work, what activities need to come before others, and how desired outcomes are achieved.

Logic models are useful in the planning stages of any new project because they require you to think through your assumptions, activities, and resources to indicate how these elements can lead to the desired intended outcomes. Without first exploring and explaining these logical linkages, your plans have a reduced chance at success and you have little opportunity to measure the cause and effect relationship between activities and outcomes (Schmitz & Parsons, 1999; Kellogg Foundation, 2004; Taylor-Powell & Henert, 2008).

Purpose

Logic models require that you thoroughly think through a proposed innovation, aligning resources with activities and activities with outcomes. Used purposively, logic models can prevent good intentions from leading to poorly conceived programs. Not only can they help ensure inclusion of the needed resources and appropriate activities, they can help you confirm with assurance the exclusion of unnecessary supports and actions.

Structure

Traditionally, logic models consist of five segments: inputs, activities, outputs, outcomes, and impact. Variations can include additional segments used by developers to suit specific needs.

Inputs are the resources available (or needed) to support the initiation of the plan. They directly support the activities, those actions and interventions at the heart of the plan that can (hopefully) produce the desired results. Together, the inputs and activities represent your key responsibilities. Inputs can be thought of as the "how" and the "what" of the plan, and the outputs, outcomes, and impact as the "why" of the plan—the results that you expect.

Outputs are immediate results that you expect to be directly produced by the activities. There should be a strong, logical connection between the activities and the outputs, such that a reader can understand your thinking and assumptions. From your perspective as a planner, this is an obvious point for midcourse corrections. If outputs are slow to materialize, then activities can be revised, times can be extended, and changes in delivery can be considered.

Outcomes are changes that can be expected over time because of increasing influence of the outputs. Outcomes represent the results of continuous improvement and eventually lead to the intended impact—the underlying "why" of the plan.

Visually, logic models are read from left to right, with each segment logically connecting to its predecessor through a series of *if-then* statements. For example, a list of needed inputs (resources) should allow you to say, *if* I gather these resources, *then* I can conduct these activities. And, *if* I conduct these activities, *then* I will achieve these outputs (results), and so on.

In exploring logic models in their simplest forms, one could argue that people plan vacations, buy cars, and make a number of major and minor decisions using logic models—even if the steps are never written down. For example, consider the thought process involved in picking a postsecondary institution. The resulting logic model might look something like Figure 1, if only in the mind of an anxious parent.

Figure 1. Logic model for selecting a postsecondary school

Inputs	Activities	Outputs	Outcomes	Impact
• Student records • Budget • Research	• Create a list of schools • Make site visits • Review applications	• Acceptance notices • Decision • Enrollment	• Education • Experience • Career decisions	• Student prepared for career choices and options

In most cases, students meet with a school official, usually a guidance counselor, to verify that their records are ready and available to be included in college application packets. With their parents and counselor, they research their school options within a budget set by their parents. From these inputs, the activities emerge—developing a list of potential schools, planning site visits, and submitting applications. Assuming success, the expected outputs—immediate results—include receiving acceptance letters, making a final decision, and enrolling. In time, the outcomes and impact should occur.

So, how should you approach the use of logic models and to what end? Schools and school districts develop new programs that require the support of the community, and proposal writers develop ideas that must convince funders to make awards. In both cases, program leaders can benefit from developing a logic model to share with stakeholders or potential funders.

The logic model becomes the visual tool for conveying the idea and showing its logical progression. Consider a simple logic model (Figure 2) for the desired outcomes of a new math program at a high school hoping to improve postsecondary enrollment for its graduates by reducing the need for remedial math. The proposers explain that with the inputs shown, they can provide the activities listed, such that the students in the program will experience the outputs, outcomes, and impact suggested in the model.

Figure 2. Logic model for developing a new high school math class

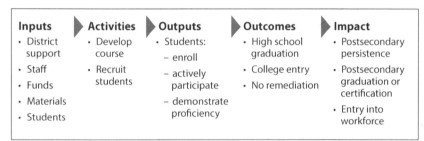

Inputs	**Activities**	**Outputs**	**Outcomes**	**Impact**
• District support	• Develop course	• Students:	• High school graduation	• Postsecondary persistence
• Staff	• Recruit students	– enroll	• College entry	• Postsecondary graduation or certification
• Funds		– actively participate	• No remediation	
• Materials		– demonstrate proficiency		• Entry into workforce
• Students				

There is no guarantee that every *if* leads to its intended ***then***; but, in this example, the authors' thought process is clear. They suggest that if the proposed math course has district support, available staff, funding, and materials, then the school staff can proceed with developing the course and recruiting eligible students. If the activities are communicated effectively, then the students will actively participate in the program and complete and submit college applications. If these outputs continue to foster the students' development, then they will graduate from high school, be accepted into college, and avoid remedial courses. If this happens, then they will persist at the postsecondary level, graduate with a diploma or certification, and be positioned to enter the workforce prepared to succeed.

Types and Uses

The logic model above is an example of an outcomes approach model, one with clear connections between the activities and the outcomes. Whether stated or implied, an outcome model usually assumes that outputs are short-term goals that can be expected to occur in the first 1–3 years or less, outcomes are longer-term goals, taking 4–6 years, and impact goals occur after 7–10 years (Kellogg Foundation, 2004). An outcomes model is especially useful in designing a long-term study because it provides you with measurable goals to assess. This model is one that is particularly useful for new programs because it can measure the short-term results in the early years of a program and begin to measure the longer-term outcomes in the later years. For example, districts that initiate new programs at the middle school level can measure 7- to 10-year results for their students as they enter postsecondary education. It can also be revisited throughout the program as a dynamic tool and can be the foundation from which theory and activity models (discussed below) are developed.

Based on the work of the Kellogg Foundation (2004), other logic models include the theory approach and the activities approach. Theory models are most appropriate in designing studies where you are trying to articulate underlying problems and assumptions about solutions. The model's structure may include problems (issue being addressed), assumptions (solution strategies), inputs (resources available), activities (based on solution strategies), and outcomes (expected results). Theory models are intended to facilitate program planning, persuade funding decisions, and demonstrate that you have researched not only the problem, but also the current literature and best practices directed at similar problems. They often address an overarching local problem (low graduation rates), provide assumptions about the target population (students), reference what is known about programs that work, and propose evidence-based activities for the population.

The activities approach focuses on implementation and may contain several activities segments, with implied links between activities as they grow across the life of a program. This type of model is helpful for managing and monitoring programs. If activities in one phase do not build upon the activities in a previous phase as planned, you can investigate the initial implementation and make adjustments accordingly. By thinking through how activities can influence each other, you can design activities to occur in phases, rather than all at once, and take advantage of these influences.

Whatever the focus of the logic model, you need to remember that it is a graphic representation of your plan and, while it can stand alone as a visual, you should plan to support it with text that is as comprehensive and specific as possible. Expand on all of the inputs, activities, and outcomes. If your inputs include money and qualified staff, then you should state how much money and how many new staff members you need. When listing activities, consider how often they occur, how many students can participate, and whether certain types of students will be targeted. Be specific about the goals for outputs, outcomes, and impacts and frame them in terms of change when practical.

For example, in expanding on "high school graduation" as an outcome, you could say "increased high school graduation" and even set a target percentage by which you expect it to increase. You can also consider whether your goal is for all students or whether you want to focus on certain kinds of students, as in "high school graduation rates of high-needs students will increase by 5 percent."

Summary

Logic models are planning tools that should not be forgotten after you start your study, nor should they be considered static. It is appropriate to revise logic models throughout the life of a project, just as it is appropriate to have several types of models with different attributes for the same project—one for planning, one for evaluating, and one for managing. Logic models can guide all three of these important project activities. Examining the notion of college and career readiness as a persistent problem can be addressed by using a logic model as the foundation for developing a comprehensive analysis plan.

Developing a Comprehensive Analysis Plan

With a firm grasp of the role of logic models in designing a study, you are ready to create an analysis plan for your study. For example, if you decide to study the effectiveness of a new program and plan for its continuous improvement, your study can also be called a program evaluation—"an individual systematic study conducted . . . to assess how well a program is working" (Small, 2012). Because one goal of program evaluation is to focus on program improvement (i.e., studying activities and assessing value), it is an effective tool for program-related decision making.

A good initial step in planning a study involves developing a comprehensive analysis plan that includes the kind of data you plan to use, the information the proposed analysis will provide, and how this information can be used to make program improvements. You should consider how you will conduct the study as well. This section expands on the earlier discussion about the scientific method and experimental design, with explicit emphasis on educational applications.

To continue with our example of college and career readiness, consider a district that hopes to improve the college and career readiness level of its students by implementing a service under the federally funded Gaining Early Awareness and Readiness for Undergraduate Programs (GEAR UP). GEAR

UP is administered by the US Department of Education to provide funds to districts and states to improve postsecondary opportunities for high school graduates. Districts use the funds to develop academic support programs for middle and high school students. Typical GEAR UP services are often related to college and career readiness: tutoring, mentoring, coaching, designated classes, counseling, parent sessions, college visits, summer "bridge" programs, and financial aid guidance. Examining how and why a district might design a GEAR UP service provides a meaningful context for the following discussion.

Descriptions, Analyses, and Evaluations

Identifying and articulating specific concerns, questions, or interests is the first step in developing a comprehensive analysis plan. Your logic model presents the desired goals for the program and the processes by which the program should help students. Formulating questions helps you decide what specific things to examine. You may want to describe your program, analyze its components, or evaluate it.

Describing a program means reporting about what is happening, and descriptive reports provide a foundation for other types of questions. Descriptive questions could include:

- How many of your students used each service? How many students of different racial or ethnic groups used the services?

- Which students in your program were on track for graduation at the end of ninth grade?

- How many parents participated in financial aid counseling sessions?

Analysis questions link causes to results. Your logic model states some relationships to test in the analysis phase, with questions such as:

- Which services or combinations of services (e.g., tutoring, mentoring, coaching, counseling) are associated with increased high school persistence and graduation? Does this relationship persist for different racial or ethnic groups?

- Are summer bridge programs associated with students being on track for graduation at the end of ninth grade?

- Is parental involvement in financial aid counseling sessions associated with students' plans for college?

Evaluations make a judgment and come to a conclusion about the value or usefulness of something. Ultimately, evaluation questions ask if your program is succeeding. In this example, are students better off for having participated in your program? Evaluations build on analyses by trying to isolate the influence of a particular component on the outcome and determining whether that component is associated with the outcome of interest. You may find an association between the summer bridge program and being on track at the end of ninth grade, but is the relationship strong enough to say that students benefitted from the summer bridge program? Evaluation questions address that. The following are examples of evaluation questions:

- Is this set of services effective in helping students graduate from high school? Is it equally effective for males and females?

- Are students who took the summer bridge program more likely to be on track for graduation at the end of ninth grade than students who did not?

- Are students whose parents participated in financial aid counseling sessions more likely to have received financial aid than those who did not?

Evaluations can be formative or summative depending on when they occur. Formative evaluations take place during the course of the program and focus on the implementation process. Formative evaluations may provide information leading to immediate corrections or revisions to the services currently offered. Consider implementation of a new online math tutoring program for students taking Algebra I. Formative evaluation questions might include: "Are students able to navigate through the program online? Do students understand the content as it is being presented online?" If answers to these questions are negative, adjustments can be made to the online tutoring program.

Summative evaluations occur after the program ends, examining retrospective data to focus on program outcomes and drawing on overall lessons that might inform future work. Here, lessons learned cannot benefit the members of the prior cohort but could benefit future students. Summative evaluation questions about the online tutoring mentioned previously might include: "Did students who took the online math tutoring program perform better in Algebra I than those who did not?" At this point, it is too late to adjust the online tutoring program for this set of students because the tutoring and algebra classes are complete. However, lessons learned may benefit future cohorts or other programs.

Both formative and summative strategies can yield information that leads to improved services. Which strategy to use is influenced by timing and what you want to know. A formative evaluation requires sufficient time to implement the service, gain information, evaluate it, and use those results to enhance the service. A summative evaluation occurs after service delivery is complete but requires access to data about events that occurred. If data about services and outcomes were not collected or maintained properly, you cannot conduct a summative evaluation.

Both formative and summative evaluation questions are based on analytic questions, which in turn build upon descriptive questions. Each type of question can be used to inform decisions about your program. If answers to your descriptive questions show that some services are undersubscribed, you could examine why students did not participate and what changes you could make to increase participation. If your analyses show that a given service is weakly correlated with high school graduation, you might find ways to improve the service or drop it and reallocate resources to services with a stronger relationship to high school graduation. If your evaluation finds that students in the program have, for example, better math scores than those who did not participate, you can use that information to expand or promote the program.

Whatever type of questions you choose to address, your analysis plan should describe the measures you will use to answer them. For example, how would you define and measure being "on track"? How would you define and measure "taking and completing college preparatory coursework"? In the latter question, would you focus on all academic subjects including foreign language? Would you limit it to math and science? You should clearly specify the questions to be answered and describe the type of information you need to answer them.

Developing a Hypothesis

What do you expect to find? Do you expect to find that your students continue to show improvement as they move through your program? Do you expect that students receiving your program's services in high school will not require college remedial courses? Do you expect that students who have received counseling about the college application and financial aid process will be more likely to apply to and attend college? Your hypothesis states your anticipated outcome and is structured in a way that will help you answer your original question. It is a prediction that can be tested and supported or rejected with data. Recall the if–then examples from the logic model discussion. For example, "If [*this is done*], then [*this*] will happen."

- If *students attend tutoring sessions in math 1 hour per week,* then they will *place out of remedial math courses in college.*

- If *we implement a graduation coach program,* then students will *graduate at a higher rate than in the past.*

- If *we compare student survey responses to college enrollment data,* then we will find that *students followed through with their postsecondary enrollment plans.*

Collecting Data

You must think through and describe the data you need to answer your questions, where the data reside, and how you can obtain the data (see Chapter 2). You also need to determine what you need to collect directly and what you need to acquire from outside sources. Some data providers require users take steps to get permission to use the data, and you can contact them to ensure that you can access the data and that you understand the permission protocols. Permission includes investigating the need for approval from an institutional review board (IRB) and informed consent. You need to take care to collect enough data and utilize the full potential of the data systems that you access.

Planning Your Analysis

Your project may offer a range of services to students, and an analysis plan should describe the treatment that the cohort of interest experienced. Your proposed question is designed to study the outcomes of your services and activities (or a select subset of services). In your analysis, you should describe the specific treatment you are studying and the characteristics of the cohort that received or is receiving the service. Some example questions to consider include:

- What services do you plan to study?

- How do students receive these services?

- What span of time do the services cover?

However, you may choose to elaborate on your questions by selecting a comparison group that did not receive the same services as your program cohort. If your hypothesis is stated as a comparison, you need to find a comparison group. These could be students from a previous year or students in schools that are similar to yours, except that they do not participate in your program. You can access student-level information from your statewide longitudinal data system (SLDS) to find a comparison group by requesting permission from the data provider. For example, if your hypothesis is "Students attending one hour of tutoring per week will place out of remediation classes in college at a higher rate than those who did not," you need to compare rates of remedial classes for students who attended tutoring with rates of students who are similar, except that they did not attend tutoring.

Once you have decided whether you need a comparison group, you need to describe how you plan to conduct your study. You should explain your design in enough detail so that it can be duplicated. Thus, you should include answers to the following questions:

- How many student records will you access?

- What kind of data do you need to answer your question?

- Can you link your student academic data to service data?

- Why are these data key to your study?

- What procedures do you use to create files for analysis?

- What methods will you use to analyze data?

- Are you using retrospective data, current data, or data you will collect in the future?

Making Program Improvements

Ultimately, the goal of the analysis is to enhance the services you provide. In your analysis plan, you should consider how you can improve your program based on the information you gain. If you find that a given service is associated with a desired outcome, how might you expand that service? What will you do if you do not find that the service is associated with the desired outcome? How often will you examine your results to see whether you should make changes to your program? Consider revisiting your logic model to help you determine if your program is progressing as intended.

Managing the Study

Finally, conducting the study requires adequate resources in terms of time, funds, and personnel. In looking at your plan, consider the following questions: How much time will it take to collect or acquire the data you need? How much time will it take to analyze the data? Do you have staff who can manage and analyze data or do you need to hire a consultant for that work? How much will it cost to collect or acquire needed data? How much will it cost to analyze data and report findings?

The answers to these questions may require you to revise your analysis plan. If you cannot do everything you would like to do, limit the study so that you can still get useful actionable information. If, for example, you do not have enough resources to follow your students past high school graduation, you may decide to focus on high school experiences and outcomes for now and do the postsecondary analysis later if funds become available. Similarly, perhaps you want to collect data from multiple sources (administrative records, surveys) but do not currently have the necessary resources. Here, you could identify and focus on which source of data is most relevant to your key research question.

The remainder of this book seeks to demystify your relationship with data, starting with how to collect student-level data, how to manage the data and create data files for analysis, how to determine the best analysis techniques for your particular data, and how to prepare your results to share with others. You will soon adopt data-driven decision making as a fundamental process for guiding the growth and progress of your program or organization.

CHAPTER 2

Obtaining Data

Introduction

Now that you have identified the question you would like to address and have developed a plan to answer it, you can think about the data you need. You may already have the data. If you are in a classroom—elementary, secondary, or postsecondary—you probably have performance data about all of your students. But, addressing some questions requires data beyond that found in a single classroom. You might need data about your students before they entered the program or after they completed it. You might need data about similar students who did not participate in the program. You might need detailed information about the services each student received, or you might want to know students' perceptions of the services.

Student-level data include information about each student in your analysis. These data permit more sophisticated analyses and allow you to account for different factors that may influence student outcomes. For example, with student-level data, you could examine whether patterns are the same for different demographic subgroups of students or whether students who received services differ from those who did not. Student-level data can be aggregated to the classroom, school, district, or state level. Aggregated data can provide information about the status of students in schools, but the richest analyses are derived from student-level data.

But what kinds of student-level data do you need? The *multiple measures* developed by Bernhardt (1998) can help you think about the types of data you need. Her work references four categories of data—demographic, performance, perceptions, and school process. Demographic data include descriptive information about course enrollment, attendance, family background, and other personal factors over which educators have no control. This information might be collected from application or registration data. Student performance data include standardized test scores, grades, and course-taking sequences and are routinely collected by schools. Such data could be obtained from a school, district, or state. Postsecondary data could be collected from postsecondary institutions or other organizations such as the National Student Clearinghouse. Perception data target what various stakeholders (students, parents, and teachers) think of the school environment and the services provided. You might collect these data in a survey, focus group, or interview. School process data focus on what schools and teachers do to get the desired results. School processes could include instructional strategies and classroom practices. Similarly, you might collect this information through surveys, interviews, or classroom observations.

Historically, some aspects of these data have resided at the school and district, but student information management systems and longitudinal databases are putting more data into a repository that protects the privacy and security of the data. You may need permission to access this information. Identifying, locating, and obtaining student data become more challenging as data files become larger and more robust. If you obtain student data, you must take care to protect students' confidentiality. Such safeguards are discussed in the *Identifying Data* and *Personally Identifiable Information* sections of this chapter.

This chapter provides guidance on deciding what measures you need to collect, finding and accessing the data you need, and developing tools to gather data that can inform your study.

Collecting Student Data

Trying to get information about events that have occurred previously can be extremely difficult and unreliable. Delaying data collection until the end of your program makes it hard, if not impossible, to get complete, accurate records of your activities and student outcomes. Having a process for routinely collecting data about all of your students gives you flexibility to conduct multiple studies as questions arise. As you solicit applications and provide services, you can collect identifying data, application data, and procedural data for the duration of your program. Likewise, during the program you can collect student participation, attitude, and outcome data. These processes can help you build a dataset that contains demographic, performance, perception, and school process information.

Identifying Data

The first step in collecting data is to obtain information that allows you to identify individual students, such as their name or identification number. With identifying data, you can link your program data to information from other sources, such as data routinely collected by the state or the National Student Clearinghouse (n.d.). Being able to identify students can facilitate collecting additional data through surveys or interviews. Ideally, identifying data should include full legal name (with nickname variations if possible), state student identification number (or Social Security number [SSN] if that is what your state uses to track students), birth date, and permanent address. You also should collect the date of the application or entry into the program so you can group students accordingly and examine results based on how much exposure students have had to the program.

Although you may collect identifying data, note that when analyzing data, you need to protect the identities of your students (see *Protecting the Privacy and Security of Student Data*). You can protect the identities of your students by creating a randomized ID number for each student that should be the same for each school year, even if the student changes schools. Use this ID number to record service use, survey responses, and any other data collected. A separate protected file should contain this ID number as well as the student's true identifying information. The file that connects the randomized ID number to the true identifying information should be kept separate from the analytic file. The person analyzing data should not be able to determine the identities of individuals in the dataset.

Application and Registration Data

Application and registration data are often good sources of demographic data. Whether students apply for a program or are automatically admitted based on program-defined criteria such as grades, you can put information that describes how the student joined the program into a data file. Application, registration, or program enrollment information includes measures of each student's status on all of your eligibility requirements, whether these requirements are academic or demographic (e.g., your program might be targeted toward high-achieving students or first-time college students). Separately, you should document how students were admitted to the program. This might include reaching certain benchmarks, such as a grade point average (GPA) threshold, a teachers' recommendation, or membership in a group, such as first-generation college students.

You might choose to add items from the application packet that provide richer data about your students' backgrounds. For example, if your program begins at the point of a natural school transition—such as the beginning of elementary, middle, or high school—you could collect information about each student's prior school experiences in the application or registration packet. For elementary school students, you could ask for information about their preschool experiences. If past academic performance is not counted in determinations of eligibility for the program, you may not need to collect detailed information about past performance on the application. However, simply knowing the identity of the prior school will make it much easier to get additional information from a district or state database if needed later.

Similarly, you might want to collect information about students' families. For example, you might want to know the relationship of the student to his or her guardian (e.g., mother and father, single parent, stepparent, grandparent, foster parent). You might collect a combination of information about the guardian's educational attainment, occupation, income, and other factors. Having insights about the student's family life may explain differences in the kinds of support families can provide.

Save application data both for those who were admitted and for those who were not admitted to the program. You may want to compare the characteristics of students served by the program to those who were not served to examine the program recruiting process. If you find that many applicants do not meet basic eligibility criteria, you could decide to modify the way you communicate the program requirements.

You may want to compare the students who were admitted to those who were not. All of the students who applied knew about the program and were interested and motivated enough to apply. Further, all applicants share certain qualities that may influence later academic success, such as motivation. The application data for students who were not accepted are potentially a rich source of information you can use to assess your admission policies. However, depending on the admission process and criteria, applicants who were not admitted may or may not comprise a valid comparison group for answering other research questions. Chapter 4 discusses comparison groups in more detail.

Service Data

Service participation data are a key component of school process measures. You provide services to help your students meet and exceed their goals. Within a program, students may participate in a variety of services, such as tutoring or counseling. When compiling data, you should not just count the number of students participating in each service, but you should record participation of individual students as well as the amount of time they spend in each activity. By recording the specific services and time spent participating, you can identify the relative influence of your services. For example, if you find that students who participated in a weekly math enrichment activity had higher grades in Algebra I than those who did not, you might conclude that the weekly math enrichment activity is effective. However, if you find no real difference in Algebra I grades between participants and nonparticipants in a summer math enrichment activity, you might conclude that you need to modify the summer activity or replace it with a weekly activity. By keeping track of which students participated in both of these services, you can gain insights into the relative effectiveness of each individual service.

You also want to collect information about how often each student participates. If you find, for example, that some students who enroll in a service miss several sessions, you would want to investigate why they were absent. Perhaps the time or location of the service is inconvenient, and students struggled to get there. Perhaps after attending a session, students decided the service was not relevant to their interests or needs. You could use that information to adjust the logistics, materials, or content of that service.

It is also important to collect attendance information to prevent incorrect conclusions because the amount of time a student spends in an activity can influence whether that activity is effective. Expanding on the example above, if the summer math enrichment activity met eight times and half of the students who signed up for it only attended once, then it may not be accurate to conclude that the summer math enrichment activity is not effective because Algebra I grades were not higher for the students who participated. You would expect that full participation would raise math scores, and if you know how often each student participated, your analyses could account for those differences. Having this participation data helps you make other decisions about services provided as well. In this example, why do half of the students only attend one time? You could interview these students to learn why they stopped attending the summer math enrichment activity. It could be due to schedule or transportation challenges, or perhaps they do not think the material is relevant to them. That information can help you improve your activity.

Additionally, you should maintain information about the process by which students select or are selected to participate in specific services. Do students decide to participate on their own initiative? Do teachers refer them? If teachers refer them, on what basis do they refer them? Does academic performance automatically place students into a service? For example, if some students are exempt from a required activity (e.g., taking Algebra I in ninth grade), why were they exempt?

Knowing the process by which students participate in various services can provide insights into your results. Suppose that students choose to participate in the weekly math enrichment activity. In that case, the most motivated and math-competent students might choose to participate, and their higher grades in Algebra I might reflect their motivation and ability independent of the enrichment activity. In contrast, perhaps teachers refer students to the weekly math enrichment activity if they think students might otherwise fail Algebra I. In that case, when you find no difference between test scores of participants and nonparticipants, you might conclude that the weekly math enrichment activity was effective because it helped these struggling students catch up to their peers. Ultimately, you need to compare the service-receivers to students most similar to them, and knowing the decision process helps you determine which students are comparable.

Summary

Consistently collecting and maintaining student-level data through applications, registration documents, and program participation can provide information that is useful for ongoing program improvement. If you have sufficient identifying information for each of your students, you can link data from your program to data from district, state, or postsecondary sources. You can also collect data through surveys, interviews, focus groups, or observations. Routinely collecting such data increases the type of questions you can address.

Accessing State and District Data Systems

Student performance measures are essential for assessing the success of certain programs and services and can usually be obtained from states and districts. Suppose you want to compare the outcomes of students receiving your program's services to outcomes of students who do not. If your program serves some students within a school, you can make within-school comparisons of those who receive services to those who do not. Making within-school comparisons requires having students who do not receive services but are otherwise similar to those who do receive services. However, if your program serves all students within a school who are eligible for free or reduced-price lunch, then you need to compare them to students who are eligible for free or reduced-price lunch in a school without your program. Similarly, if you are studying a whole-school reform program, you need to compare your students to those in other schools.

To examine outcomes of students in other schools, you often need to obtain data from your state or district. To track student outcomes over time, you need longitudinal data that include multiple years. With longitudinal data, you can examine your students' academic work before and after participating in a service or program. With consistently collected state-based or district-based data, you can compare your students to similar students in other schools who do not have the benefit of participation in your program.

This kind of information would help you address questions such as:

- How do students in your program compare to similar students in different schools who do not participate in a comparable program?

- How many students in your program are on track to graduate high school at the end of their freshman and sophomore years compared to similar students in another school that does not have a comparable program?

- Are achievement gaps smaller for students receiving your services than for similar students who do not receive your services or comparable services?

Statewide Longitudinal Data Systems

Many states have created robust statewide longitudinal data systems (SLDSs). With longitudinal data, you can track an individual student's academic progress and not only examine proficiency within a year but also academic growth over time. Table 2 provides an example of data from a longitudinal database that contains information about student performance on end-of-grade exams in middle school.

Table 2. Longitudinal dataset tracking students' progress through middle school

Student	6th grade math score	6th grade reading score	7th grade math score	7th grade reading score	8th grade math score	8th grade reading score
Rosa	67	75	62	74	82	80
Derrick	74	72	70	68	66	64
Julia	78	75	77	76	79	75

The Data Quality Campaign (DQC), founded in 2005 as a national advocacy group, monitors and reports on each state's progress toward building systems to manage student data that can generate information useful for improving student achievement. One of the DQC's first actions was to identify and describe what it referred to as the 10 essential elements of SLDSs and to support states in their efforts "to improve the collection, availability, and use of high quality education data" (DQC, 2006). The DQC provides information about each state's progress in collecting high-quality longitudinal student data and policies for using such data. Information contained on the DQC's website[1] can help you understand your state's status in these general areas.

The DQC provides a national platform for state directors and policy makers to talk, share, and learn from each other as they build their longitudinal data systems and implement the elements deemed to be essential for a robust SLDS. The essential elements describe features needed in a fully functional SLDS for it to provide specific longitudinal student-level information, such that it is possible for states to:

- follow students' academic progress as they move from grade to grade;

- determine the effectiveness of specific schools and programs;

- identify consistently high-performing schools so that educators and the public can learn from best practices;

- evaluate the effect of teacher preparation programs on student achievement; and/or

- focus school systems on preparing a higher percentage of students to succeed in rigorous high school courses, college, and challenging jobs (DQC, 2006).

As described, SLDSs include far more information than just test scores. With SLDSs, states create student identifiers that allow you to follow a student who changes schools and to link information from various data sources, such as school enrollment, course taking and completion, scores from multiple assessments, attendance, and dropout status. SLDSs also include students' demographic data and may include information about their participation

---

[1] http://www.dataqualitycampaign.org/

in programs, such as special education or the free and reduced-price lunch program.

Your state's department of education may have enhanced its data system through the SLDS Grant Program or through another initiative. The federal SLDS Grant Program has awarded competitive, cooperative agreement grants to states since 2005. These grants provide funds over a period of 3 to 5 years to foster the successful design, development, and implementation of longitudinal data systems. Through the six rounds of funding (2005, 2007, 2008, 2010, 2012, and 2015), 47 states, the District of Columbia, Puerto Rico, American Samoa, and the Virgin Islands have received at least one SLDS grant (US Department of Education, n.d.). You can review different states' objectives in creating their SLDS online.[2] Additionally, most states provide some policy and funding support to develop data systems and to create publicly available reports about schools and students (DQC, 2013).

Student-Level Data Collected by States

Although all states have included certain key elements in their SLDSs, they differ in the kinds of data they collect, the way they link files from other sources, and the extent to which they permit stakeholders to analyze that data. Before requesting data from your state's department of education, you should become familiar with your state's data collection and reporting processes.

By 2011, most states had incorporated the essential elements into their data systems (Table 3). All states have a statewide identifier and maintain annual student-level enrollment, graduation, and dropout status. Additionally, all states maintain information on student participation in some kinds of school programs and have a state audit system to assess data quality and reliability. All but one state maintains information on students who are not tested under the state's accountability system (DQC, 2011).

---

[2] http://nces.ed.gov/programs/slds/stateinfo.asp

Table 3. Number of states adopting new Data Quality Campaign actions

DQC's 10 essential elements	Purpose	Number of states*
A unique statewide student identifier	Follow individual students	52
Student-level enrollment, demographic, and program participation information	Study relationship between demographics, participation, and performance	52
The ability to match individual students' test records from year to year to measure academic growth	Provide diagnostic information to teachers and principals	52
Information on untested students	Study patterns in student subgroups	51
A teacher identifier system with the ability to match teachers to students	Study teacher preparation programs and teaching assignments, especially with regard to low-performing populations	44
Student-level transcript information, including information on courses completed and grades earned	Study relationship between course-taking patterns and college/work readiness	41
Student-level college readiness test scores	Study the transition from high school to postsecondary	50
Student-level graduation and dropout data	Follow students who drop out of school	52
The ability to match student records between the P–12 and postsecondary systems	Provide high schools with feedback on the success rates and course-taking patterns of graduates	49
A state data audit system assessing data quality, validity, and reliability	Monitor and ensure accuracy and validity of data	52

*Includes the District of Columbia and Puerto Rico
Source: Data Quality Campaign (DQC), 2011

The America COMPETES Act of 2007 and the American Recovery and Reinvestment Act (ARRA) of 2009 led to the development of federal guidelines for SLDSs, which absorbed most of the recommendations put forth by DQC. Given that most states had made progress on these elements, DQC shifted its focus to recommending 10 actions that states should take to further this development (Table 4). These actions include linking K–12 data with early learning, postsecondary education, social services, and workforce data; developing governance structures to guide data collection, sharing, and use; and creating reports using longitudinal statistics to guide system-wide improvement efforts. Most states have developed data repositories, created reports using longitudinal data, and developed governance structures to guide data collection.

Table 4. States taking additional steps to develop statewide longitudinal data systems (SLDSs)

DQC's 10 State Actions	Number of states accomplishing the action by 2015
Link state K–12 data systems with early learning, postsecondary education, workforce, social services, and other critical agencies	19
Create stable, sustained support for a robust SLDS	41
Develop governance structures to guide data collection, sharing, and use	42
Build state data repositories (e.g., data warehouses) that integrate student, staff, financial, and facility data	46
Implement systems to provide all stakeholders with timely access to the information while protecting student privacy	11
Create progress reports with individual student data that provide information that educators, parents, and students can use to improve student performance	35
Create reports using longitudinal statistics to guide system-wide improvement efforts	45
Develop a purposeful research agenda	41
Promote educator professional development and credentialing around the access, analysis, and use of data	18
Promote strategies to raise awareness of available data and ensure that all stakeholders can access, analyze, and use data appropriately	33

Source: Data Quality Campaign (DQC), 2015

Finding State-Specific Information

Once you have a sense of your state's general policies for data collection and analysis, you can turn to your state's department of education website. This website can serve as a tremendous resource for learning more specifically about the kind of student data the state maintains. Under the Every Student Succeeds Act, each state is required to produce annual report cards with information about student achievement. State department of education websites post this information, which can by searched by district and school. Each state produces annual report cards that provide information about student achievement. The school report cards and other annual reports describe how each state defines certain measures. For example, a measure of "days absent" may refer to excused absences, unexcused absences, or both.

You can also search your state's department of education website for evaluation reports conducted or commissioned by your state. These reports provide information about the kind of data the state policy makers are using to address certain kinds of questions. In addition to tracking the information about the data, you should note the names of any report authors, who may become helpful contacts for you.

To find evaluation reports, you can use search terms such as evaluation, research, data, or statistics. You can also search within specific divisions or programs of the department, such as accountability, academic reform, or dropout prevention. Because states develop their own approaches to organizing and presenting materials, you have to be creative as you search these websites.

Accessing Your SLDS

Once you have determined what data you need to facilitate project improvement, you will need to determine how to access the data. As noted above, the DQC website presents actions each state is taking to facilitate effective data use. States can facilitate data use by implementing the following practices: (1) a governance structure to clarify the procedures for sharing data, (2) data repositories that store and integrate data from multiple sources, (3) systems for providing stakeholders with access to information, and (4) practices to ensure educators can use the data properly. Not all states have taken these actions yet, so you have to plan accordingly. For example, if your state does not have procedures for sharing data, you need to spend more time developing a memorandum of understanding or a memorandum of agreement for data use. A memorandum of understanding is a general statement of understanding between two parties, but it is not a legally binding contract and is not appropriate if funds are to be exchanged. Here, both parties outline and agree to expectations and responsibilities. A memorandum of agreement is a legally binding agreement. If the state you work with does not have procedures in place, you could use the memorandum of agreement templates from states that do have them as a guide. If your state does not have a repository for linking data from multiple sources, you need to include someone on your team with sufficient computer programming skills to accomplish that.

Again, you can get more specific information from your state's department of education website by searching for terms such as data access, requesting data, or data use. Additionally, your searches for data may yield information about data access, evaluation tools, or descriptions of best practices for data use.

Ultimately, you need to contact staff in the department of education to initiate this process. Possible contacts include staff within the office of research, education reform, or strategic initiatives as well as authors of the evaluation reports located earlier. Particularly in a state that does not have clear procedures for facilitating effective data use, you may need to make several contacts before locating the appropriate person.

School District Data

In some cases, you may prefer to get student performance data from a school district. Some districts have established robust data collection processes, often gathering information beyond their state requirements. To determine the kinds of information your district collects and whether they have data-sharing policies, review the district's website to learn about their data practices and data availability. Districts that collect more extensive data files typically have a division of research.

The steps for developing a plan to use district data are similar to those for state data, including searching the district website for the types of data they collect, the statistics they report regularly, and the kinds of evaluations that have been conducted using these data. When you understand the kinds of data you want to use, you should contact a district official to discuss next steps. Some districts collect extensive data but may not have processes for sharing data. Districts that do have procedures in place may post these processes on their website. If a district does not have such a process in place, you can suggest that the district use your state's policy, provided your state has a policy in place. If not, examine the policies of a different state or district that shares data and use its requirements as an example.

Data from Other States

Some study questions may require acquiring data from multiple states. For example, if your program is delivered in multiple states, you may want to examine program outcomes by state. To test the success of a program across multiple states, you need student data from every state in which it operates.

Using data from multiple states is challenging. State end-of-grade or end-of-course exams may not be comparable. A study of course taking and progression has to ensure that course titles and methods of flagging honors or remedial classes are consistent. States may define other student characteristics, such as exceptionality, differently as well. Ensuring the data are comparable takes extra resources.

In this instance, rather than getting data from other SLDSs, you may consider partnering with service providers in multiple states and collaborating on the study. Working with partners in other states who are familiar with their own state data may be more efficient than working on your own. Whether you form a partnership or do all the data analysis yourself, taking care to consistently examine the same kinds of data across sites makes it possible to examine student enrollment, service use, and outcomes across states.

Accessing Postsecondary Data

Postsecondary data provide other measures of student performance after high school. Although you have created a database with basic data about secondary school experiences on all your students, it may be valuable to examine their experiences after high school. This section provides an overview of points to consider when developing a plan to access postsecondary data.

Sources of Postsecondary Data

Two main sources of postsecondary data could help you examine your students' outcomes or the effectiveness of your program: SLDSs and the National Student Clearinghouse. State-level data systems vary by state in terms of development, content, and accessibility. Although most states that have postsecondary systems include basic information such as enrollment, additional variables differ significantly among states. The National Student Clearinghouse is a nonprofit organization that provides information about student enrollment and degree completion for a fee. Another source of information is the National Student Loan Data System, which is the US Department of Education's database for student aid. It provides an integrated view of the Direct Loan, Pell Grant, and other US Department of Education programs.

Analyzing Postsecondary Data

With postsecondary data, you can examine whether your students entered a postsecondary program of study after high school. With robust postsecondary data, you can compare college-going rates as well as various aspects of postsecondary attendance for students who participated in your program, took advantage of your services, or enrolled in your education program with those who did not. With such information, program directors could address several different kinds of questions, such as:

- Where did your former students attend college?

- How long after high school graduation did they enroll in college? Did their transition from high school to college occur within a certain time frame?

- How long were they enrolled in college?

- Were they required to take remedial courses?

- Once enrolled in college, did they transfer?

- Did they graduate from college? Did they earn any postsecondary credential?

- Which services are correlated with postsecondary enrollment after high school?

- Which services are correlated with college graduation? Which services are correlated with earning a postsecondary credential other than a bachelor's degree?

- Do any of these patterns vary by demographic subgroup, particularly for students who are underrepresented in postsecondary education?

Postsecondary Data in SLDSs

SLDSs that connect K–12 data, postsecondary data, and, ultimately, workforce data are still in the planning stages in most states. Whereas many states have developed robust primary and secondary SLDSs containing information about students enrolled in kindergarten through high school, such longitudinal data systems are not common in the postsecondary sector. Thus, the availability and quality of state-level postsecondary data vary widely.

State-level postsecondary data systems generally include only data on public institutions and not private colleges and universities. Some states have postsecondary data from only one institution of higher education, while others have data from several institutions, institutions within a sector (such as public 4-year institutions or community colleges), or all institutions in the state. For example, Florida's education data system includes all public postsecondary institutions in the state, and these student-level records can be linked to relevant K–12 data. In contrast, in North Carolina, the University of North Carolina's General Administration maintains a state-level unit record system with records for each student enrolled in any of the 16 public, 4-year universities in the system, while the North Carolina Community College System Office maintains a similar state-level unit record system that includes records for each student enrolled in any of the 58 North Carolina community colleges. Currently, these two data systems are not linked to each other or to the K–12 data system, although plans for their merger are under way. They also do not include information about students enrolled in any of the private colleges in the state.

A further complication is that currently many state postsecondary data systems are not longitudinal, but rather are "snapshots" of student data at particular points in time. And while most state-level postsecondary data systems contain enrollment information and graduation information, the systems vary greatly in the student outcome data (e.g., courses completed and grades) they include.

Finding Your State's Postsecondary Data System

If your state has linked K-12 to postsecondary data through an SLDS grant from the National Center for Education Statistics (NCES), you can learn about it through the NCES website.[3] If a state has not developed an SLDS that includes comprehensive postsecondary data, then you can try to obtain information through state-level unit record data systems for postsecondary education. The State Higher Education Executive Officers Association (n.d.) conducted a study of postsecondary state-level data systems, which is available on its website.[4] By using the interactive report *The State of State Postsecondary Data Systems,* you can determine whether a particular state has a state-level postsecondary unit record system, the postsecondary institutions that contribute data to the unit record system, the data elements that are collected, and the agency that is responsible for the system.

National Student Clearinghouse Data

If your state does not have a postsecondary data system that you can access or if you want to look at postsecondary outcomes across institutions and states, you could use the StudentTracker for Outreach service from the National Student Clearinghouse.[5] The Clearinghouse provides a fee-based matching

---

[3] http://nces.ed.gov/programs/slds/stateinfo.asp

[4] http://www.sheeo.org/projects/state-postsecondary-data-systems

[5] http://www.studentclearinghouse.org/about/

service, and its database contains information provided by more than 3,600 postsecondary institutions. The Clearinghouse collects data representing approximately 94 percent of students[6] enrolled in postsecondary institutions in the United States and provides information about enrollment by semester, institution in which a student is enrolled, and type and date of any degrees received. To obtain data from the Clearinghouse, you must provide students' names and birthdates to the Clearinghouse for their staff to match against postsecondary student unit record data. The Clearinghouse will then provide you with a dataset containing the student-level postsecondary information.

Effective Methods for Collecting Data

You may need to collect additional data to obtain information about items rarely found in these other sources, such as student perceptions and school processes. Before collecting data, you should clarify exactly what information you need to know and how you will use it. For example, did a new attendance policy increase attendance at a program activity? What do parents think of a new nutrition plan in the school cafeteria? Is the newly implemented block schedule proving beneficial to all students or only to specific groups? You also need to consider how you will use the data to make decisions about your program. Will you improve or eliminate a program? Will you report your findings to a governing board or funder? Or will you implement a new strategy? You can review your analysis plan (described in Chapter 1) in considering how to answer these questions.

The attendance question requires simple data collection. You merely need to count the absences for the present and previous years, and collecting such data is straightforward. You may not be able to credit the new policy with any improvements in attendance because other school or student factors may influence attendance rates. However, you can describe trends in attendance. Another example involves determining how parents feel about a new nutrition plan in the school cafeteria. Assessing parent views or attitudes about any school activity requires interacting with the parents. You might ask parents to complete surveys sent home with students or offered online, or you might conduct interviews and focus groups. This kind of data collection requires

---

[6] Students could be missing in the Clearinghouse data if they did not attend any postsecondary institution, if the student attended a postsecondary institution that does not report to the Clearinghouse, if the student opted out of data sharing, or if the name or birthdate used for matching with Clearinghouse records was incorrect (Dynarski et al., 2015).

time, effort, coordination of schedules, development of questions, and staff to gather, organize, and analyze the data. In another example, if you wanted to explore the impact of a new block schedule on various groups of students, a range of data collection activities could apply. Your questions could focus on perceptions, school processes, or student performance. To understand perceptions, you might have students complete surveys or meet face-to-face with interviewers, either alone or in focus groups. To understand school processes, observers could document student engagement during classroom observations. To understand the schedule's influence on student performance, you might compare student attendance and performance under the new schedule to their attendance and performance under the old schedule. To determine whether students with specific characteristics were affected differently, you might incorporate demographic measures to see if perceptions and performance differ by student characteristics, such as gender, race/ethnicity, or socioeconomic status.

Survey instruments, interviews, and observations are used to obtain data about school processes and stakeholder perceptions, which may not be routinely collected. Designing survey instruments, interviews, and observation protocols requires in-depth understanding of the program's logic model as well as the research questions you want to address. Whether your data collection is for a single purpose or is a phased activity in a comprehensive evaluation plan, you need a working knowledge of the purpose and intention of the data collection efforts so that your questions are precise and your sources of information are appropriate. In this section, we explore ways to align the best data collection tool with the desired information.

Surveys

Typically, surveys are a standardized way to get information from a sample of people. With a survey, each individual is asked the same questions. Usually these questions have multiple-choice or rating-scale responses that can be scored and reported quickly, although surveys can include open-ended questions. Surveys are an easy way to reach a large number of potential respondents and yield results that are quantifiable (e.g., 33 percent of students think a great teacher is one who makes the subject interesting). In the school context, surveys are a method to obtain measures of school processes and stakeholder perceptions. On surveys, you can ask questions about the processes of instructional strategies and stakeholder perceptions of those activities. Students encounter surveys attached to standardized tests when test administrators seek data on student perceptions or learning opportunities. Teachers complete surveys for supervisors and textbook vendors. Schools and districts often survey parents to gather community perspectives about current programs and upcoming plans.

Paper and pencil surveys often involve a "bubble sheet" that respondents complete and submit for mechanical reading and output. When sent in the mail, the response rate is unpredictable because people may forget to complete and return it; however, when people have the opportunity to answer the survey in a controlled setting, such as a classroom, the response rate is higher because people can complete and submit it right then. Online tools such as Survey Monkey allow researchers to create and distribute surveys and monitor results without special web technology skills. Such websites offer predesigned survey templates and assist developers in designing questions and analyzing results. Some vendors, such as Youth Truth and Snap Surveys, offer a standardized set of questions designed to determine student perceptions of their engagement and classroom culture. Vendors might administer surveys, compile data, and provide online reports for schools and districts. Multiple choice survey questions for students might look like those in Table 5.

Table 5. Sample multiple-choice survey questions

Which choice best describes your plans after high school?
a) 4-year college
b) 2-year community college
c) Technical certification
d) Military
e) Enter the workforce

In what after-school extracurricular activities do you participate (choose as many as apply).
a) Academic club (such as French or math club)
b) Arts club (such as band or dance)
c) Service club (such as Rotary or Civitans)
d) Sport (such as basketball or volleyball)
e) Other

Following best practices for online surveys from Couper (2008) and Dillman and others (2008) ensures that the user interface and design meet all standard online requirements and provide a highly usable tool for respondents, which improves data quality and reduces respondent burden. These best practices call for implementing a single survey item on each page, a practice that has the following benefits:

- It produces significantly less missing data than when multiple survey items are on a page (Peytchev, 2009). Having a single survey item on each page enables "paging" rather than "scrolling" through the survey. Scrolling presents more questions on a page and permits the user to scroll freely up and down the page. Paging instruments typically have fewer items with missing data (Peytchev et al., 2006).

- It allows people to skip questions if they are not appropriate based on prior responses. For example, if Q1 is "Do you eat in the school cafeteria?" with response options:

  a. Every day
  b. Some days
  c. Never

  a response of c (never) could result in Q2, "How would you rate the food in the cafeteria?" being skipped.

- If you have access to the necessary technical expertise or are using a vendor with such expertise, surveys can be adapted for mobile devices. For example, teachers can ask students to access a survey during class via three options—laptop, smartphone, or tablet—thus minimizing burden and guaranteeing a high response rate for the survey. Figure 3 presents an example of a survey that has been optimized for mobile devices. With this technology, an auto-detect feature can usually be incorporated that determines whether a respondent has accessed the survey from a mobile device.

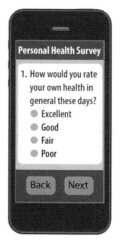

Figure 3. Sample mobile device survey question

If you are directing a project that offers professional development to teachers on standards-based lesson and curriculum development, you might have questions about what they think is important in lesson design. An online rating scale survey question for these teachers may look something like Figure 4.

Because they are easy to distribute, surveys are effective tools for gathering data from treatment and control groups for studies requiring this type of comparison. In one of the examples above, you might ask the question about students' plans after high school in a school with an academic enrichment program and in one without such a program. Researchers might be interested in determining the influence of the program and could compare student responses from the two schools.

Figure 4. Sample online rating scale survey question

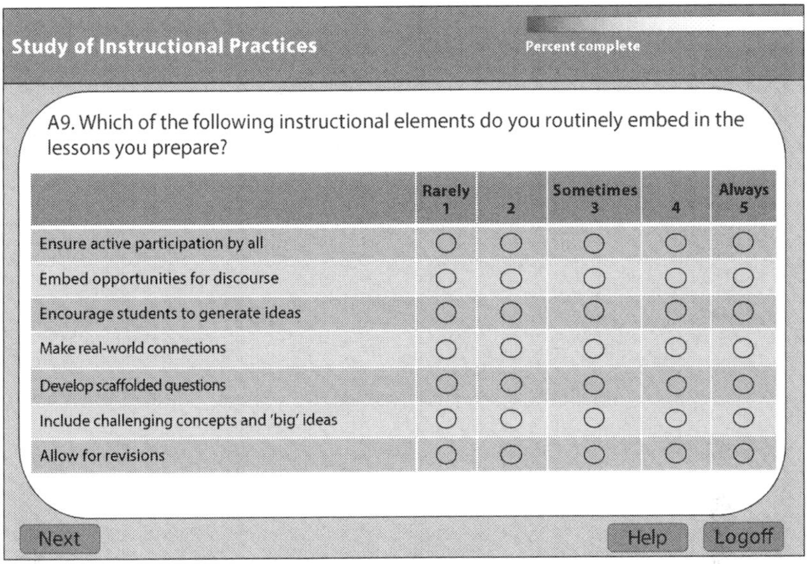
Study of Instructional Practices

Percent complete

A9. Which of the following instructional elements do you routinely embed in the lessons you prepare?

	Rarely 1	2	Sometimes 3	4	Always 5
Ensure active participation by all	○	○	○	○	○
Embed opportunities for discourse	○	○	○	○	○
Encourage students to generate ideas	○	○	○	○	○
Make real-world connections	○	○	○	○	○
Develop scaffolded questions	○	○	○	○	○
Include challenging concepts and 'big' ideas	○	○	○	○	○
Allow for revisions	○	○	○	○	○

Next Help Logoff

Interviews and Focus Groups

Interviews and focus groups are other ways to get school process data and perception data. Here, questions are more open ended rather than in a survey. Interviews and focus groups are time consuming to design and costly to implement and analyze. Also, the data require sorting and categorizing because they are not quantitative results that can be manipulated mathematically. However, the open-ended structure of interviews may give you new insights into the school processes and perceptions. People may say things that you would not have thought to include in a survey.

Traditional interviews are conducted in person or over the phone, the former being preferred (but costly) to allow the interviewer to gauge respondents' reactions and the need for follow-up or further probing questions. Phone interviews are less personal but necessary when time and money are factors in the data collection process. Neither are desirable for a large sample and lend themselves more readily to purposive sampling or studies where the interviewees are preselected and identified as essential to the data collection.

Regardless of the method used, interviews require you to keep accurate field notes, use audiotape when permitted, and collect useful artifacts (e.g., lesson plans, school handbooks) when possible. Interviews tend to focus on gathering opinions, such as the following questions:

- How did your school decide to implement this program?

- What kind of professional development do teachers get?

- What other kinds of professional development would help your teachers implement this program?

- What kinds of support do you receive from the district? From the state? From the community?

- How do you think this program benefits students? In your school, what is the greatest benefit?

- What challenges has your school faced in implementing this program?

Interviews also permit the researcher to follow up on responses in ways not possible with a survey. One useful application of interview data is to inform the development of survey questions. Interviews can uncover important background information that can be investigated with a survey. For example, if the current school program being studied replaced a long-standing, popular program, questions about the previous program can be included in the interview. This is why some studies schedule survey data collection after interviews.

You can consider focus groups as a group interview, but they are much more focused on gathering opinions and perceptions than facts. Focus groups rely on the group dynamic to encourage active and enthusiastic participation and allow for unexpected responses. Focus groups should include a manageable number of members (6–10) and be built around a small number of questions (5–6).

Fields such as marketing and advertising have long used focus groups when developers need to test responses to new products. As the name "focus group" implies, questions need to be focused and goal specific. For example, in a project-based learning school, a focus group could seek to determine students' reactions to the program. Meaningful questions could include:

- What do you like most about project-based learning?

- What is one thing you would change about project-based learning?

- What class offers you the most interesting project-based learning activities? (Ask for examples.)

- What was the biggest adjustment you had to make to succeed in a project-based learning class?

The success of both interviews and focus groups depends on the skill of the facilitators. Experienced facilitators know how to keep the conversation on track, control dominant speakers and encourage hesitant ones, and probe for further information. Success also depends on the ability to analyze effectively the data obtained from interviews and focus groups using qualitative procedures.

Interview and focus group data can be analyzed using different techniques. One process involves putting notes into a series of matrices to identify themes. (See Miles et al. [2014] and Saldaña [2013] for more information.) For example, responses to the question, "What do you like most about project-based learning," might include working with other people, more meaningful topics, less boring, and figuring things out myself. An analyst could create columns for each type of response and then tally the number of people who gave each response. With interviews and focus groups, people can give many responses, and this method allows an analyst to capture all of them. Someone who said "working with other people" and "less boring" would be counted for each response. Beyond analyzing data with this type of method, an analyst could use software such as Atlas.ti to identify patterns in focus group and interview data.

Classroom Observations

Classroom observations provide another way for you to get data about school processes. With this method, an observer watches the class to assess elements of instruction based on best practices in improving student success. With classroom observations, you could address topics such as content, student cognitive engagement, activities involving inquiry and critical thinking, instruction/formative assessment, use of technology, and classroom culture. Observations usually focus on the extent to which students engage in classroom learning and activities and the kinds of instructional practices used by teachers to engage student problem-solving skills. You might also use observation data to provide feedback to teachers so they can make decisions about improving their classroom practices.

Classroom observations are best performed by those familiar with the pedagogical content knowledge specific to the academic subject under question. Observations are also often mandated by district policy as a means of documenting teacher practice for performance purposes. These often focus on classroom management, organizational skills, and student engagement.

When performing classroom observations, you can use a hard-copy format for taking notes (for ease of flipping between pages) or an electronic format via laptop or tablet. You can easily transfer handwritten notes to an electronic instrument and send the notes to a data collection site via e-mail or a secure file transfer protocol. Most observation instruments contain both rating scale assessments and open-ended responses. This approach yields quantitative data that you can manipulate as desired and qualitative responses for content analysis. These data can be used to verify instructional practices and can be cross-referenced with information captured in the surveys, interviews, and focus groups.

Observations provide direct access to students and teachers and an opportunity for trained observers to assess the social climate of the classroom by noting actual interactions among students and teachers, the level of student engagement, the appeal and rigor of activities, and the ways in which teachers encourage and ensure student participation. Observation data provide a lens through which teachers can compare their own interview data (perceptions) to observation data from their classroom (what is documented).

The caveat with regard to developing observation protocols is to practice restraint in deciding what is valuable. You might consult the national standards in your academic area to review best practices—increased student dialogue, improved integration of technology, better questioning techniques—and embed these in your observation instrument.

Protecting the Privacy and Security of Student Data

When collecting student data, you must take care to protect the privacy and security of these records. This section summarizes the key concepts and internal procedural controls related to the privacy and security of student data records, as discussed in the US Department of Education's Privacy Technical Assistance Center Statewide Longitudinal Data Systems (SLDS) Technical Briefs (Seastrom, 2010a, 2010b, 2010c).

Personally Identifiable Information

The Family Educational Rights and Privacy Act (FERPA) of 1974 was enacted by Congress to protect the privacy of student educational records. Types of personally identifiable information (PII) include direct and indirect identifiers. Direct identifiers provide information that is unique to the student or the student's family, such as name, address, SSN, and unique education-based identification numbers. Indirect identifiers include information that can be combined with other information to identify specific individuals. Examples of indirect identifiers include gender, race or ethnicity, religion, date of birth, place of birth, mother's maiden name, education information, and specific activity or program participation.

As defined in FERPA 2008 regulations, PII for education data and student education records includes but is not limited to:

- Direct identifiers
  a. Student's name
  b. Name of the student's parent or other family members
  c. Address of the student or student's family
  d. A personal identifier, such as the student's SSN, student number, or biometric record
- Indirect identifiers
  a. Student's date of birth, place of birth, and mother's maiden name
  b. Information that is linkable to a specific student that would allow a reasonable person in the school community to identify the student with reasonable certainty (for example, if your ninth grade class had only two Hispanic females, a person familiar with the school who saw a school report about ninth grade Hispanic females could draw conclusions about them)
  c. Information requested by a person who may know the identity of the student to whom the education record relates

Data Protections

Conducting research requires taking steps to ensure the rights of study participants are protected. "Research" is defined by US Department of Health and Human Services (HHS) regulations as "a systematic investigation, including research development, testing and evaluation, designed to develop or contribute to generalizable knowledge" (45CFR46.102(d)). A systematic investigation incorporates data collection and analysis to answer study questions. It is designed to draw general conclusions and apply knowledge gained to groups other than those involved in the study itself. Tallying the number of students who use your coaching service is not "research," but analyzing the relationship between coaching and high school graduation and publishing a report suggesting that coaching helps disadvantaged students complete high school are considered research. Research projects might compare alternative processes; collect information beyond that which is routinely collected for a program; assign people to different groups (treatment or comparison) to identify the best practices; conduct pre- and post-comparisons; gain results that are intended to benefit people outside the project's population; and share results to benefit others through publication in a journal or public presentation at a professional meeting.

An IRB or committee for protection of human subjects can review your plan for data collection and analysis to determine whether these activities count as research and need to be formally reviewed. If you obtain data from a state or district, you may be required to go through an IRB review, and the state or district may have an IRB process in place. If you partner with a university, you can often rely on its IRB.

Some kinds of data collection and analysis are exempt from IRB review. These analyses include studies involving tests, surveys, interviews with adults that have no linkable identifiers, studies where disclosure of results does not put the participant at any risk, and studies using existing, publically available data or data recorded in a way that they cannot be linked to individuals. The exemption status is determined by the IRB of record.

When collecting and using data about human subjects, you must follow guidelines to make sure people are treated properly. In 1981, HHS and the Food and Drug Administration issued regulations governing the conduct of research involving human subjects. The HHS regulations are provided in Title 45, Code of Federal Regulations, Part 46.[7]

Basic ethical principles for collecting and using data about human subjects are summarized in the Belmont Report (HHS, 1979), which focuses on three basic principles:

1. **Respect for persons.** Anyone participating in a study should be treated with courtesy and respect. They should be informed of the study, and they have the right to consent to participate in it. For example, if completing a survey about classroom goals is outside a teacher's scope of

---

[7] http://www.hhs.gov/ohrp/humansubjects/guidance/45cfr46.html

work, she has the right to choose whether to do the survey. A principal should not coerce her into doing it. She should understand how the information will be used and consent to do it. Children may use your services, but they are not obliged to participate in the study. Children are not old enough to legally consent to participating, but their parents should consent on their behalf. If program participants do not consent to being part of a research study, then you would exclude their data from that kind of report. You can still use data to monitor program implementation, which is not considered research.

2. **Beneficence.** The research should benefit participants, and you should minimize any risks to them. Although research on education has fewer obvious risks than, say, medical research, any risk should be minimized. For example, answering survey questions about bullying may distress someone who has been the victim of bullying. An IRB would help make sure the questions are not written in a way that seems to blame the victim and that when responding to the survey, students understand their answers will be confidential.

3. **Justice.** Reasonable procedures should be administered fairly. This means that you should have an impartial process to select whose data are collected and used. You cannot decide to get data only from students you like or the ones you think will give good responses. The selection process needs to be objective and linked to your study questions, so you might collect data from all free-lunch students in geometry or all science teachers in the school.

Whether or not your use of data constitutes research requiring a review, you can use these principles as guidelines to ensure that people are treated fairly.

Data Stewardship

If you use student data, then you have legal and ethical responsibilities for protecting PII in student education records and for making sure that student data are used appropriately. Seastrom (2010a) defined data stewardship as an organizational commitment to ensure that data in education records, including PII,

- are accurate, complete, timely, and relevant for the intended purpose;
- are collected, maintained, used, and disseminated in a way that respects privacy and ensures confidentiality and security;

- meet the goals of promoting access to the data for evaluating and monitoring educational progress and educational programs; and

- meet the goals of assuring accuracy to ensure that decisions relating to an individual student's rights and educational opportunities are based on the best possible information.

As discussed in the next section, you can take specific steps to satisfy these elements of data stewardship.

Internal Procedural Controls to PII

The SLDS Technical Brief *Data Stewardship: Managing Personally Identifiable Information in Electronic Student Education Records* (Seastrom, 2010b) describes specific internal controls that assist in managing personally identifiable data. Although this document focuses on SLDS, techniques that can be applied to any student data collection include the following:

- assigning new unique student identifiers to replace students' PII in longitudinal electronic data systems;

- implementing procedures for workforce security to ensure that only authorized staff members are given access to personally identifiable student records;

- ensuring that access to each student's education record is available on a "need-to-know" basis;

- developing operating rules for the conditions of use, such as rules concerning permissible uses and prohibiting unauthorized uses, procedures for protecting PII, and procedures for ensuring destruction of copies of records at the end of a period of authorized use; and

- planning for possible data breaches by establishing procedures for reporting known or suspected breaches, analyzing the causes and impact of breaches, and notifying affected individuals.

A more detailed discussion of each of these steps is provided in the subsequent section.

Assigning New Unique Student Identifiers

As noted in the Identifying Data section, following the experiences and outcomes of students as they move through the education system requires you to have a unique student record identifier, which allows student data collected from different sources and different points in time to be linked together. You can create a randomized unique student identifier that is not related to the student's SSN or other personal information. Only a limited number of staff should have access to the secured sensitive information and information about the process for creating the randomized identifier or permission to use the unique student identifier to link data from different sources.

Implementing Procedures for Workforce Security

Procedures for workforce security include the use of security screenings, training, and binding confidentiality pledges (Seastrom, 2010b). You are recommended to perform security screenings, such as background checks, for new employees and for staff members whose job duties include accessing PII in student record data. You should also provide regular data security training for employees and cover a variety of topics, including:

- roles and responsibilities (the student information each employee is authorized to access and what is considered appropriate and inappropriate use of the data);

- legal and regulatory requirements that apply to the access and handling of PII;

- internal security practices and policies (where data can be accessed, use of passwords and firewalls, and how to detect and respond to breaches in security); and

- penalties for violating the laws, requirements, or internal security policies.

Finally, you should have each person working with data sign a pledge or Affidavit of Nondisclosure. The pledge should indicate that the data user acknowledges the purpose, restrictions, and appropriate uses of student record data; promises to protect each student's PII; is aware of relevant laws, regulations, and rules; and understands the penalties for violations.

Establishing Need-to-Know Access to Student Record Data

Data access needs will vary across employees. Although a few employees, such as those who set up the data system, will need full access to the data, most will only need access to select data fields. Limiting each employee's access to need-to-know data fields, data records, and data files will reduce the risk of inappropriate disclosure of PII. Policies and procedures should outline who is authorized to access the student record data and the conditions under which they may be accessed and released (Seastrom, 2010b).

Developing Operating Rules for the Use of Student Record Data

Once you have authorized data users and analysts and granted them access to student education records, they must abide by established rules and procedures for using the data consistently with the terms agreed to in the Affidavit of Nondisclosure. Security controls for using the data involve access and use procedures and electronic security.

Data Access. Policies should specify where people can physically access student records. Access to the most sensitive student information should be limited to a secure location, such as a locked room that is accessed only by authorized users or on a nonnetworked computer. Access to the files should be protected by strong passwords. Although less sensitive information could be accessed on a wider range of computers, data files including PII should not be stored on public computers that might be used by staff who are not authorized to access the student record data. Also, identified data should not be put on a portable medium such as a CD or flash drive.

Firewalls can be used to protect a server, network, or individual computer from viruses and unauthorized access. A firewall refers to a network device that blocks certain kinds of network traffic, forming a barrier between a trusted and an untrusted network. It protects networks from unauthorized access while permitting legitimate communications to pass. If data that contain PII are transferred to an external location, secure networks and electronic encryption should be used.

Using Student Data for Reporting Aggregate Statistics. When combining or aggregating student-level data, you should use techniques to protect the identity of individual students. For example, if reporting student outcomes for different student subgroups results in groups with a small number of students, someone might deduce the identities of people in those groups. You can establish a minimum reporting size, such as at least three members in a group, to protect confidentiality. You can report tabulations with zero cases because they have no data to protect. Seastrom (2010c) provides a detailed discussion of approaches to protecting identifiable student information in aggregate reported data.

Electronic Data Security. All of the surveys and data you collect should reside on servers that meet security standards. You can find best practices for establishing secure protocols through the US Department of Education's Privacy Technical Assistance Center's website, which includes a toolkit with issue briefs and checklists.[8]

Plan for Possible Data Breaches

Every privacy and data protection plan should include a response plan for the appropriate handling of a breach of PII. The *Guide to Protecting the Confidentiality of Personally Identifiable Information* (McCallister et al., 2010) includes a detailed discussion of how to handle data breaches. In particular, you should develop a clear description of what constitutes a breach and inform all staff members who are authorized to access sensitive data. Staff members should also be informed about the immediate steps that need to be taken in the event a security breach occurs or is suspected.

Summary

Student-level longitudinal data systems are essential to policy, program, and instructional decisions. However, the use of such data systems should be balanced with appropriate protections for student record data. That is, those who use student data have ethical and legal responsibilities to respect the privacy and confidentiality of each student's PII. Implementing internal procedural controls to protect the privacy and security of student records mitigates risks related to the intentional and unintentional misuse of student data.

---

[8]   http://nces.ed.gov/programs/ptac/Toolkit.aspx

CHAPTER 3

Measuring and Managing Data

Introduction

No data come to you in perfect shape, complete, and ready for analysis. Also, a single data source rarely provides all the variables needed to examine a particular research question. As a result, you often need to use multiple data sources to obtain all the variables of interest for your studies. When working with student longitudinal data, additional years of data, such as academic data or program participation data, become available. The data contained in these different data files need to be merged to create a single analysis file. This chapter describes the data management process and suggests data checks that you can perform to avoid the common problems associated with managing data and ensuring its quality.

Longitudinal student datasets map student progress over time by merging data from multiple periods. With these large data systems emerging in many states, it is possible to define and follow cohorts of students and compare their progress through school. This allows you to track the relationship between program services and student achievement. For example, if you know what academic support services students used in their middle and high schools and their college enrollment and remediation needs, you can analyze the influence of the support services on students' college enrollment and participation experiences.

Managing your data requires that you understand the big picture-view first—what data you need to answer your questions of interest, evaluate your program, or respond to school administrators. After you determine your needs, you can inventory what data you have or can access to determine what additional data you need to track down and what sources can provide what you need. For example, at the school level, you may have student-level data on attendance and grades, but you may have to access the district database to find state or national test data. In addition, some of your students may have attended a summer program, and you need to contact the summer program to get student performance data. If you are tracking students who have graduated, you may want to access the National Student Clearinghouse to retrieve college enrollment and completion data.

Defining and Measuring Variables

Appropriately defining and measuring variables of program activities and outcomes are essential to program evaluation. If measures are not appropriate, then the findings may not adequately address your study question. Suppose you want to examine whether students who engage in project-based learning in mathematics classes understand the relevance of this subject, but the end-of-course exam scores are your only outcome measure. These test scores would inform you about their performance in class, but they do not tell you students' perceptions of the subject and do not directly answer your question. Therefore, you need to carefully determine the concepts you need to measure and obtain the appropriate variables for each. You can define variables in two ways:

1. Conceptual definitions explain the concept you are trying to measure

2. Operational definitions explain how you will measure the concept

Conceptual Definitions

A concept is an abstract or general term referring to an idea, person, thing, or event. Concepts include terms like *motivation, instructor, math program,* or *college entry*. Although these terms are generally understood, they can be defined and measured differently to match the focus on the study question. For example, college entry commonly means enrollment in any postsecondary institution following high school. However, based on your study questions, you may want to focus on 4-year colleges or only on full-time enrollment, or you may want to include students who take college classes while in high school.

Some concepts, like motivation or college readiness, are more abstract, cannot be measured directly, and require care in crafting definitions. For example, the concept "high school transition success" could be defined by academic behaviors, perceptions of school climate, or psychological functioning. Each definition requires a different measurement. If your study question only focuses on academic achievement, you may measure "high school transition success" with test scores and grades. However, if your study question focuses on attitudes and psychological function, then a measure of only academic achievement would be incomplete. You may need survey responses to measure these dimensions of success.

The research question identifies the key concepts involved in a research project. For example:

- **Research question.** Does participation in college access program services affect the likelihood that participants will enroll in college?
  - **Key concepts.** Service participation, college enrollment
- **Research question.** Are achievement gaps by race smaller for students receiving your services than for students who are not receiving services?
  - **Key concepts.** Achievement, race, service participation
- **Research question.** Does rigorous course taking in middle school improve the likelihood that students will graduate high school?
  - **Key concepts.** Rigorous courses, high school graduation
- **Research questions.** Do students in this program feel more prepared for college or careers than their peers?
  - **Key concept.** Feeling prepared

Converting Concepts to Variables

Once you identify a concept's dimensions, you can develop variables for the dimensions. Variables for each concept can be defined in more than one way. From the examples given, the service participation variable could identify whether a student participated in a service at all, the number of times a student participated in a service, or the types of services a student used. *College enrollment* variables could include type of college (4 year versus 2 year), attendance status (full time versus part time), and timing of college enrollment (within 6 months of high school graduation versus later). *Achievement* variables could include end-of-grade or end-of-course exams, specific grades, or GPA. *Race/ethnicity* variables could use standard US Department of Education 7-category definitions (American Indian or Alaska Native, Asian, Black or African American, Hispanic, Native Hawaiian or Other Pacific Islander, White, and Two or More Races). You may want to collapse those categories into "underrepresented minority" versus "other" students, in which case, you could put American Indian or Alaska Native, Black, Hispanic, Native Hawaiian or Other Pacific Islander, and Two or More Races in the "underrepresented minority" category and "Asian" and "White" in the "other" category. *Rigorous course* variables could include taking Algebra I or advanced English by the end of eighth grade or the number of credits earned in advanced classes. *High school graduation* is a concrete concept, requiring simple variables such as "yes" or "no" and a date. *Feeling prepared for college or career* could include survey data with questions asking students to rate the level of agreement or disagreement with statements like "I understand the steps I need to take to apply to college."

How you choose to define variables depends on the most important aspects of your research questions—and on the availability of data. It is important to develop variables that represent the concepts they are intended to measure. The more precisely the variable represents the concept it intends to measure, the more valid the evaluation will be. However, if certain kinds of data cannot be obtained, then you should get the closest measure you can. You may need to shift the way you define the concept. For example, in the question about whether college access programs increase the likelihood of college enrollment, you may want to know about full-time or part-time enrollment. If you cannot obtain data on enrollment intensity, you cannot define enrollment on that basis. Two examples of the process of converting concepts to variables are provided in Table 6.

Operational Definition of Variables

Once you have conceptually defined variables and specified what you want to measure, you need to operationally define them—that is, determine how to measure the variables. Doing this requires reviewing the data you have collected and acquired to determine how data elements can best measure your concepts.

Level of measurement pertains to how the variables are classified for analysis. There are four levels of data: nominal, ordinal, interval, and ratio. The level of measurement determines the appropriate types of analyses (Engel & Schutt, 2013). Nominal and ordinal variables are categorical variables, used for classifying and counting, and frequency distributions are the typical method for analyzing them. Interval and ratio variables are numeric and used in more complex statistical analyses.

Nominal variables group observations into discrete, mutually exclusive, and exhaustive categories. All observations should fit into one, and only one, category. These categories are not ranked: one category is not considered better than another. Race and gender are nominal variables. Each student should be in one of the race categories and one of the gender categories. Nominal variables are the most basic level of measurement. This level of measurement tells you whether two observations are alike or different (e.g., these two are alike on this dimension, as they are both boys; they differ from those two girls).

Table 6. Examples of the process of defining variables

Key concepts	Dimensions	Variables
RESEARCH QUESTION: Does participation in program services affect the likelihood of participants enrolling in college?		
Service participation	Receipt of service(s)	Receipt of any service
		Receipt of financial aid assistance
		Receipt of college application assistance services
	Duration of participation	Number of months in the program Participation through high school graduation
	Intensity	Number of hours of services received Number of services received
College enrollment	Type of college	Enrolled at 4-year college
	Attendance status (full time or part time)	Enrolled full time at 4-year college
	Timing of enrollment	Enrolled full time at 4-year college in the fall immediately after completing high school
		Any enrollment at a college by the age of 25
RESEARCH QUESTION: Does rigorous course taking in middle school improve the likelihood that students will graduate high school?		
Rigorous coursework	Completion of rigorous courses	Completion of any advanced course
	Subject area	Completion of algebra by end of eighth grade Completion of advanced English by end of eighth grade
	Intensity of rigorous course taking	Number of credit hours earned in advanced classes by end of eighth grade Number of advanced courses taken by end of eighth grade
High school graduation	Type of credential	Receipt of regular high school diploma
	Timing of graduation	Receipt of regular high school diploma within 4 years of ninth grade enrollment

In analyses, nominal variables are used to determine the number of cases, the mode type, and the equity of representation. For example, you can use them to determine the percentage of blacks, whites, and Hispanics receiving a given service. You can see whether the percentage of Hispanics receiving a service represented the school's percentage of Hispanics.

Ordinal variables also classify observations by type and are mutually exclusive and exhaustive. However, ordinal variables are rank ordered, and one category is regarded as better than another. Letter grades are an example of an ordinal variable. An A is better than a B, which is better than a C. Scaled survey questions in which people report their attitudes can yield ordinal variables. For example, to address the research question concerning whether students in this program feel more prepared for college or careers than their peers, you might use the survey question, "I know the steps to take to apply to college," and ask students to respond using a 5-point scale (ranging from 1 = "strongly disagree" to 5 = "strongly agree"). Strongly agreeing that one knows the steps for a college application is better than not being sure, which is better than strongly disagreeing with that statement. Although these categories are ranked, there is not an exact numerical relationship between categories. You can say that "strongly agree" is better than "agree," but you cannot say that "strongly agree" is twice as good as "not sure."

Interval variables classify observations by type and rank order and require that differences between levels of the variable be equal (for example, temperature or intelligence as measured by IQ), but the meaning for 0 is arbitrary. The difference between 75 and 80 degrees is the same as the difference between 40 and 45 degrees, but 0 degrees does not mean there is no temperature.

Ratio variables are similar to interval variables but have a true zero starting point (number of students, number of questions correctly answered on an exam). With a ratio variable, a value of zero means there is none of that element at all. Interval and ratio variables can be used to calculate means, standard deviations, and correlations.

Interval and ratio variables can be converted to ordinal or nominal variables. For example, the number of questions correctly answered on an exam could be collapsed into grades of A to F or pass-fail. Ordinal and nominal variables cannot be converted to interval or ratio variables.

Reliability and Validity

Ultimately, you want your measures to be reliable and valid. Reliability means that a measure is consistent—it works the same way every time. If a phone is reliable, you can use it to make and receive calls from anywhere at any time. A reliable educational assessment should work the same way every time. It should not matter whether a student takes an exam in the morning rather than the afternoon or on a Tuesday rather than a Friday.

Suppose you used information from Algebra I and advanced English classes to study the influence of rigorous course taking. Whether you offered the algebra exam via pencil and paper or online, you would expect a similar distribution of scores regardless of how students took the exam. If, on average, online scores were much higher than pencil and paper scores, you would wonder whether these forms of algebra assessments were reliable. Similarly, if you have two people grading advanced English exams, and, on average, one grader gave students much higher marks than the other, you would want to examine whether the grading process was reliable. Within an assessment, you would expect each item to be reliable. If your algebra exam had three questions requiring students to solve linear equations, you would expect that students who understood the concept would be able to answer all three questions assuming that they were of equal difficulty. If most students could answer the first two questions but none could answer the third question, you would conclude that the last question was not reliable.

Validity means that the measure is accurate. It measures what you want it to measure. Content validity means that a measure captures all dimensions of a construct. An end-of-course advanced English assessment that only included questions about topics covered in the last month of class would not have content validity as it does not capture all of the topics covered in class. Criterion validity means that a measure corresponds to an external measure in the way you would expect. If students who got good grades in algebra all failed the end-of-course exam, you would wonder about the validity of those grades. Do they adequately measure student proficiency? If measures are not valid, their use will not accurately address your study question.

Summary

In developing variables, you define them first conceptually and then operationally. The conceptual definition captures the key elements of your research question and logic model. This process identifies what you want to measure. The operational definition specifies how you will measure it.

The different levels of measurement (nominal, ordinal, interval, and ratio) determine the kinds of analyses you can conduct. Regardless of the level of measurement, measures should be reliable and valid.

Data Quality

Evaluating whether a program meets its goals requires having high-quality, reliable data. If data are not reliable, you may draw conclusions that are not correct. Most problems with data quality arise from data entry errors, misunderstanding of variable definitions, and lack of access to data. Simple data entry errors can occur due to typographical errors (e.g., numbers are transposed, the wrong box is selected, or a name is misspelled). Variable definitions cause data quality problems if they are not standardized or if definitions change over time. For example, days absent might mean all days absent, excused absences only, or everything except suspensions, which are tracked separately. Without a clear definition of ***days absent***, an analyst might erroneously interpret absences. If the definition changes from all days absent to only excused absences, it may appear that students' days absent had declined over time, when only the definition had changed. Throughout the data collection and analysis processes, you can take steps to ensure that you have high-quality data. You can develop strategies to prepare for data collection, collect data, confirm collected data, and manage data merging and analysis.

Preparing for Data Collection

Preparing for data collection requires defining variables and creating data collection systems. If you work with schools, those schools already have systems in place to track students' academic progress. You need to learn as much as possible about their data collection strategies and variable definitions. If your schools rely on the Common Education Data Standards initiative, a national collaborative effort to develop common data standards, then you can refer to that website as well.[9] Beyond data routinely collected by schools, you may want to analyze information about participating in services or student and parent opinions of services or of college going. You need to carefully define the values of the data to be collected and everyone on your team must understand the data definitions.

---

[9] https://ceds.ed.gov/

As much as possible, you want to create an automated data collection system. You may be able to get regular updates with student academic data from the school. You may be able to use Web-based surveys or reports of service use so that responses do not have to be transferred from paper to the computer—although if using a paper data collection process is the only way to get data, then you can plan to check the results. You should have automated processes to back up data as well.

Collecting Data

Throughout the data collection process, you should develop and maintain a data dictionary, a document that describes each variable. Examples are illustrated later in this section. This document is a resource for all staff who work with the data, write reports, and present information about the program. Having a centrally located, well-maintained document that accurately describes the data helps all staff use appropriate definitions.

Collecting data using the most refined categories enhances data quality. Even if you want to report school-level results, you need to collect data at the student level rather than simply tracking the totals. You can aggregate results in the analysis phase. In addition, you should keep categories as basic as possible. If you want to report the percentage of ninth graders who pass Algebra I, collect the total number of ninth graders and the number who passed Algebra I. You can calculate percentages at the analysis phase. If you only have percentages, you may not be able to double check or adjust if there are subsequent data corrections.

If you develop surveys to collect data, make sure that your answer choices are comprehensive, specific, and clear. In developing questions, make sure respondents can accurately answer them. As an example, if you only want one response per item, make sure that the response options are mutually exclusive; otherwise, include an option to "check all that apply." You can pilot test a survey or have staff review it to get feedback on the questions. The following examples show solutions for problems with survey questions.

Resolving Problems with Survey Questions

Examples of problem questions and strategies to overcome them follow.

1. How many times have you talked with your parents about college options this year?

   Problem: Students probably will not know the exact number of times they have talked with their parents over a year.

   Solution: You get a more accurate answer by asking how many times in the past week or month they have had this conversation. Alternatively, you could give broad categories of answers, such as

   - Never

   - One or two times

   - Three to five times

   - More than five times

2. How did you feel about the college counseling program?

   Problem: Students will answer this question in different ways, using different words to describe different kinds of feelings. To analyze data, you will need to review and recode the answers.

   Solution: Ask specific questions about more feelings and reactions. Focus on what is most relevant for implementation of the program. Examples include the following:

   - After the college counseling program, I feel more prepared to apply to college.

     ○ Strongly disagree

     ○ Disagree

     ○ Agree

     ○ Strongly agree

   - In terms of time required, I thought the college counseling program was

     ○ Too long

     ○ Just right

     ○ Too short

3. Which services have you used? (Check as many as apply).

- Counseling
- Tutoring

Problem: If your program offers more services than this, your students will not have the option to report about them. A student who has not used any services does not have the option to say so.

Solution: Make sure the list is comprehensive by adding options such as

- Counseling
- Tutoring
- College visits
- Meeting with mentors
- Saturday academy
- Other, specify_____
- None

Note that 10 options are a good limit for a survey question so that respondents can keep track of the choices. If you have too many options, you can break out separate questions, such as focusing only on one-on-one services versus group services or high school academic services versus college planning services.

4. Have you participated in tutoring?

- Yes
- No

Problem: If most of your students participate in tutoring, this question does not let you distinguish among students.

Solution: Make the question more specific. Examples include the following:

- How often have you participated in tutoring?

  o More than once per week

  o Once per week

  o Once or twice a month

  o Once or twice this year

  o Never

- In which subjects have you been tutored (Check all that apply.)?

  o Math

  o English

  o History/social studies

  o Science

  o Other subject

  o None

5. Do you like this program? If not, why not?

   Problem: This is a leading question, and students may not feel free to answer honestly.

   Solution: Making the question more specific and giving options may help students feel more comfortable in answering the question. Examples:

   - What do you like about this program? (Choose as many as apply.)

     o It is helping me succeed in my classes.

     o I feel more prepared for college.

     o My teachers help me.

     o Other _____

   - What challenges do you face in participating in this program? (Choose as many as apply.)

     o Schedule

     o Transportation

     o Time commitment

     o Activities don't seem relevant to me

     o Too much extra work

     o Other _____

Data Confirmation

Once your data are compiled, you can take steps to double check the variables. First, you need to look at frequencies of all categorical measures and averages of all numerical measures to make sure that data entered are within the appropriate range. For example, if your program serves high school students, and the frequency of your "grade" variable showed that you had first graders, you would want to identify those students and correct their grade level. If you found that the school had a dropout rate of 100 percent, you would want to review and correct the dropout data. Similarly, if you found that only 10 percent of the eighth grade students had taken the required end-of-grade English exam, you would need to investigate the assessment data.

When linking data, you need to check the extent to which students have consistent information reported. For example, if a student is listed as eligible for free lunch in one source but not in another source, you must determine which source is more reliable and use that one. As you develop rules for linking data, you should document all of these rules in the data dictionary.

If your program takes place in multiple schools, you should compare important measures across schools. So, if one school's data differ greatly from all others, you should review the data collection process at that school.

Summary

Through careful processes of preparing for data collection, collecting data, and confirming the validity of collected data, you can ensure that your data are of high quality, which makes your results more reliable.

Merging Data Files

The data merge process combines datasets that have the same or related observations but different variables. You may want to combine a student-level data file that contains academic achievement information for the students who received services from your program with a student-level data file that contains program participation information for the same group of students. Both of the data files contain student-level data for a single group of students, but the data files contain different information about these students. The data merge process combines these two data files to create an analysis file that includes one record for each student, and each student record includes both the academic achievement and program participation information.

Data appending is a second reason to combine datasets. Data appending is the process of combining files with different observations but the same variables. If you acquire academic information for a new cohort of students that needs to be added to your master data file, you can append it to a master data file that contains the same academic information for prior student cohorts. In this example, you want to add similar observations for new students, rather than additional variables, to the master data file.

When combining data files, you need to be clear about whether you are adding variables or adding observations because a different process is required for each. This section focuses on merging datasets.

Types of Data Merges

With student data, there are three common types of merges: (1) one to one, (2) one to many, and (3) many to one. The one-to-one data merge involves combining two student-level data files on the same group of students. Each data file has the same number of student records, and the students included in the first data file match the students included in the second data file. In contrast, the one-to-many data merge is used when you want to merge hierarchical data. An example includes merging a data file that contains school-level information onto your student-level analysis file. In this case, information about a particular school is merged onto each of the student records in your master data file associated with that particular school. It is a one-to-many data merge because you are matching one school record to many student records. You may also encounter a many-to-one situation when you have multiple records (e.g., attendance at multiple tutoring sessions) for one student.

Longitudinal Datasets

A longitudinal student dataset is created by merging data from multiple periods, making it possible to define cohorts of students and follow their progress through school. With this approach, you can examine the relationship between program services and student achievement. For example, knowing about the students' middle school academic performance, the middle school services they used, and their ninth grade academic performance, you can determine the extent to which middle school services aid in the transition to high school.

Unique Identifier

A unique identifier is a variable or set of variables that uniquely identify each observation or each student. For example, if a school provides academic data for students served by your program, the file might include a standardized student identification number, name, and birth date for each student.[10]

---

[10] Different data systems use different identifying measures; you should adjust the approach depending on the kinds of identifying information.

Ultimately, you want to create a file with one record per student that includes all the associated data in consistently named identifying fields.

Matching on all three criteria simultaneously is most likely to give reliable matches, but data discrepancies mean that records for the same student might not match. You must review the mismatches and make decisions about which ones actually match. Another approach is to match data using the student ID, then compare the other individual criteria to make sure that the match is correct. *Note that these decisions are judgment calls and you should always document the rationale for any such decisions.* The following are some strategies for resolving discrepancies in different kinds of identifiers.

Student ID

Most schools and school districts have a unique standardized student identification number attached to each student. If so, this ID is a robust tool for matching. Even with such a tool, data entry or scanning errors may cause a problem like this:

- "14368" was scanned as "14868"

- "15995" was entered as "15959"

If only one digit is off, or if two numbers are transposed, and other identifiers (such as name and birth date) match, you may be able to assume that these match.

Name

Sometimes you will encounter data discrepancies involving the way names were entered into the dataset. Spanish symbols or apostrophes in one source but not another and lower-/uppercase differences can cause major problems when merging. For better match results, remove all symbols from names and convert to all upper case or lower case in both sources before merging datasets.

Last names might be misspelled or have scanning errors:

- "O'Brien" and "Obrien"

- "Rodriguez" and "Rodriquez"

First names might be misspelled or have scanning errors:

- "Matthew" and "Mathew"

- "Lamarr" and "Lamaar"

Some people use nicknames:
- "Elizabeth" and "Beth"
- "Robert" and "Robby"

Some people use their middle name for the first name:
- "John R" and "J Reid"
- "Mary K" and "M Kristen"

If not already set up in separate fields, you can split the name variable into first, middle, and last names and see how well the records match, considering each component of the name. If all other identifiers and last name match, you can look at the discrepancies among first names. Then, if all other identifiers and first name match, you can look at the discrepancies among last names. You may find that you are able to consider counting the following as matches:

- The last name matches. The first initial of the first name is the same in each record. Here, "Mathew" can be considered a match to "Matthew."

- The last name matches. The first initial of the first name in the first record is the same as the initial of the middle name in the second record. Here, "M Kristen" can be considered a match to "Mary K."

- The last name matches. One of the first names is a nickname for the other. Here, "Elizabeth" can be considered a match to "Beth."

- The first name matches. If last names differ only by one letter, you might consider that a match. Here, "Rodriguez" probably matches "Rodriquez" and "Thompson" probably matches "Thomson."

Note that in these cases, you can confirm the match by comparing birth date or school/district code. And you should always document your reasons for making these judgments.

Birth Date

As with the student ID, birth dates will not match if a record has a data entry or scanning error:

- "12/18/1997" should be "12/19/1997"

Additionally, month and day might have been transposed so that
- "8/4/1998" becomes "4/8/1998"

If only one element (month, day, or year) differs or if the month and day are transposed, you may decide that these records match.

Although student unique identifiers are necessary to link data sources, they are PII and as such require stricter handling guidelines because of the increased risk to an individual if the information is compromised. To protect students' PII, you should not retain unique identifiers that are based on students' PII on your data analytic file. Rather, you should create a separate file that includes students' PII and the unique student identifier that you have created that does not include PII, store this file in a secure location, and use it only when merging data files. (See Chapter 2 for a more detailed discussion of strategies for protecting students' PII.)

Pre-data–Merge Checks

Conducting a data merge requires knowing the structure and contents of each data file. You can avoid common problems associated with data merges by performing the data checks discussed below before performing the merge.

Check the Observations

First, inspect the observations included in the data files to be merged. Do the data files include the same student records or do any of the files include a unique identifier value that is not in the other data file(s)? For example, suppose you want to merge the data file that includes students' academic information with the data file that has students' participation information. The academic data file includes a student record that has a unique identifier value of "20562," and a student record with this value is not included on the participant information data file. The resulting data merge file will include the "20562" student records and the variables from the academic data file will have values, but the variables from the participant data file will have missing information (see Table 7). In such cases, you need to decide whether you want to retain or drop this record when merging the data files.

You need to check whether duplicate unique identifier values exist in one or more of the datasets. An example of duplicate observations includes the academic dataset having two records with the value of "20356" for the unique identifier, whereas the participation data file has only one record with a unique identifier value of "20356." Duplicate observations can produce unexpected results when merging data files, especially if you are unaware of their existence. If duplicates exist, you need to determine whether the duplicates are valid or

Table 7. Data merge results from two different student records

	Participant information			Academic information	
Unique ID	First service year	Gender	Ethnicity	Grade 8 math score	Grade 8 reading score
10058	2010	Male	White	375	383
10279	2010	Male	Hispanic	312	273
10288	2011	Female	Black	289	291
10452	2011	Male	White	271	254
10915	2012	Female	Black	320	301
20244	2012	Female	Hispanic	364	343
20331	2012	Female	Asian	228	261
20562				296	304

due to errors in the data. If duplicates are due to data errors, then you must decide which one of the duplicate records to retain and which to drop.

Finally, you should check to see if there are records that have a missing value for the unique identifier variable(s). For example, if both the participation data file and the academic data file include a record with a missing value for the unique identifier, the merge process will match the two missing values and create a single student record in the merged data file, even though the missing value record from the two files might not represent the same student.

Check the Format of the Unique Identifier

Another important data check is to determine whether the unique identifier variable is formatted the same way in both data files. Specifically, does the unique identification variable have the same length and type attributes (e.g., is it a numeric or character variable) in both data files? You can perform a data merge when the lengths are different, but unexpected results can occur. If the variable has different type attributes in the two data files, the statistical software program will likely stop processing and issue error messages when you try to merge the data files. An example of different type attributes includes having the unique identifier defined as a character variable in the academic data file and defined as a numeric variable in the participation data file. To avoid potential problems, make sure the unique identifier variable is of the same type and has the same length in both data files.

You should try to convert the unique identifier variable to a character variable rather than a numeric variable because data are more likely to be stored or read in unexpected ways when they are numeric. For example, if the unique identifier variable is defined as a numeric variable and some of the student records have values that include leading or trailing zeroes (e.g., "05689" and "48950," respectively), the software program may drop the zeros (e.g., "05689" becomes "5689" or "48950" becomes "4895"). Another potential problem with having the unique identifier variable defined as a numeric variable is that the program could unexpectedly round the number (e.g., "5689" becomes "5690"). Changing all unique identifiers to character variables eliminates the danger of these problems.

Check the Format of Other Variables

Confirm that all of the data sources define variables in the same way. If not, you need to reconcile differences. Sometimes discrepancies result from different approaches to coding variables. For example, if course grades are coded alphabetically in one file (A, B, C, D, and F) and numerically in another file (4 = A, 3 = B, 2 = C, 1 = D, and 0 = F), you need to recode the variable on one file to match the variable used in the other file.

In other cases, discrepancies occur due to policy changes. For example, when states modify an end-of-course exam (e.g., Algebra I), the scale of the scores and their values may not mean the same thing from one year to the next. Here, it would not make sense to compare these measures unless you can obtain a conversion table showing how each new score corresponds to each old score. Without such a guide, you cannot standardize these measures. If this is the case, then you need to analyze the scores from earlier years separately from those of the following years.

Check for Common Variables on Both Datasets

As noted previously, a data merge combines data files that have different variables. In some cases, the data files that you want to merge will have one or more common variables. For example, both the academic and participation data files might include an attendance variable. When these data files are merged, only one value for attendance will be retained (the value retained depends on which data file was listed first in the merge statement of your computer code or a default selection in your software package). When merging data, this common attendance variable will present particular problems if the value for the attendance variable is not the same across the two data files. For example, suppose that the attendance variable on the academic data file represents the students' attendance at school, whereas the attendance variable on the participation data file represents the students' attendance at services offered by your program. You need to decide whether you want to drop one of the attendance variables before the data merge or whether you want to include both on the merged data file.

To include both academic attendance and program participation attendance information on the merged data file, you need to rename the attendance variable in at least one of these data files. For example, in the academic data file you can rename "ATTENDANCE" to "ATTENDANCE_ACADEMIC." You can also rename the attendance variable in the participating data file to "ATTENDANCE_SERVICES." The merged data file now includes both attendance variables and the meaning of each is clear.

Check Longitudinal Data Files, Rename Variables That Occur in Multiple Years

Some variables will be included in each year's data. If so, you need to rename the variables to indicate the relevant time period, such as year. For example, if you have a variable indicating the number of days a student was absent each year, you can name the variable "DAYSABS2013" to indicate the number of days absent in 2013–14 and "DAYSABS2014" to indicate the number of days absent in 2014–15. You must rename the variables before you merge the data; otherwise, you will not be able to tell which year is associated with the days absent variable after the merge.

Check for Observations or Variables Not Needed for Analysis

In some cases, there are variables in the data files to be merged that are not necessary for your specific analysis. If so, you can drop these variables before merging in order to simplify your data and allow for faster data processing. For example, suppose the academic data file includes records for every student enrolled at the school. If the analysis only includes students who entered seventh grade during fall of 2012, then you can drop the student records that do not meet this criterion. This prevents unwanted observations or variables creeping into the analysis and allows the analysis software to run more efficiently.

Conducting the Data Merge

There are several statistical software packages (e.g., SPSS, SAS, Stata) that can be used to merge data files. A discussion of specific statistical programming code used to complete the data merge is beyond the scope of this book; however, references for data merge programming code for a few of the statistical software programs indicated are provided in the references section.

Regardless of the statistical software package used, you need to sort your data files by the unique identifier or identifiers. If the data files do not have the unique identifier sorted in the same order, the statistical software package will likely stop processing and issue an error.

Before conducting the data merge on all observations included in your data file, you can conduct the merge on a subset of the data to make sure the merge produces the expected results. Once you have confirmed that the records from the two data files are merging correctly, you can perform the data merge for all observations.

Post–Data Merge Checks

Once the data merge is completed, you need to inspect the resulting data file to ensure that the merge was successful. For example, you should check the number of variables and observations in the final dataset to make sure that the numbers are the same as expected. Also, you should select a sample of observations and make sure the information from the source files matches the information in the merge data file. For example, if the student record with a unique identifier value of "25987" has "male" listed for the gender variable on the participation data file, but "female" listed for the gender variable on the merged data file, the data merge combined the wrong records (i.e., mismatched records). You will need to recheck the structure and contents of your data and the programming code you used for the data merge to determine what went wrong.

Summary

Analyses often require the use of variables from different data files. Merging data is the process that combines variables from different sources into a single analysis file. For data files to be merged, they must share a unique identifier (e.g., a student identification number). To ensure that observations in the data files are combined correctly, several data checks must be performed before merging the data so that you are familiar with the structure and contents of each data file. You must make sure that the unique identifier variable or variables in the data files have the same format (i.e., length and type attributes). Additionally, the unique identifier variables need to be sorted in the same order in the data files to be merged. Finally, after performing the data merge, you need to check the merged data file to make sure that the results are as expected.

Documenting the Process

Conducting a study of a program or service may involve various people and data sources. A longitudinal analysis requires repeating data collection, analysis, and reporting activities in subsequent years. Documenting the process as it develops makes it easier to collaborate with others, write reports, and repeat or modify data collection and analyses later.

Data Sources

It is helpful to have descriptions of each data source in one place. The structure of the dataset is the framework for the kinds of analyses you can conduct. You should have addressed many of the questions below in planning the study and acquiring data. For each data source you use, you should include the following kinds of information:

- **Source of the file.** Did your team collect the data? If not, what organization provided the data? What data sharing arrangements do you have?

  Any report using the data needs to identify the source of the data. If another party collected the data, you should include the original name of the file. Using the proper name for the secondary dataset makes future requests easier.

- **Frequency and timing of data collection.** How were the data collected? When were the data collected? Were data collected at the beginning of the year? At the end of the year? How often were data collected? Annually? At the end of each semester? Only once? When does the organization collecting the data release it for others to use?

If certain data are collected more than once a year, you need to know whether the final record is the most complete or whether the files should be combined to complete data. For example, if attendance is reported at the end of the fall and spring terms, the spring "days absent" measure might include fall and spring days absent, or it might only include spring days absent. In that case, you need to combine data from both files to get the total.

The timing of the data collection is crucial because studying the influence of your program or service requires having outcomes that occurred after students received the service. If, for example, you are examining the influence of a positive behavior program on student disciplinary infractions, you need to have infractions data that were collected subsequent to the positive behavior program.

If you are using data collected by another party, you need to allow time for them to prepare the data for release. For example, in preparing end-of-course exam scores for an SLDS, the state needs to process the test results, create its own reports, and even share reports with the state board of education or other state organizations before releasing the data to other groups. Such a process could take several months, and you need to build that time into your schedule.

- **Who is included in the file?** Is it all students within a district or school? Is it students within a certain grade or classroom? Is it only students who received program services? Is it students within a given demographic group, such as those eligible for free or reduced-price lunch? Is it a sample of students, such as those who responded to a questionnaire?

The students included in the file affect whether you can have a comparison group.

- **What is included in the file?** What variables are in the file? How are they defined?

The organization providing data may provide a codebook, or you may have to develop one yourself. If you collect data, you need to develop your own. Documentation should include a list of variable names, definitions, and values (see Table 8).

Table 8. Data collection codebook sample entries

Variable	Values
ETHNIC	Student's race/ethnicity I = American Indian A = Asian B = Black H = Hispanic M = Multiracial W = White P = Native Hawaiian or Other Pacific Islander
ALG1ACH	Algebra I end-of-course achievement level 1 = Insufficient mastery 2 = Inconsistent mastery 3 = Consistent mastery 4 = Superior performance
PLANS	Plans after high school A = Seek employment B = Enlist in military service C = Enroll in a trade school D = Enroll in a community, technical, or private 2-year college E = Enroll in a 4-year college F = Undecided G = Other
TUTORING	Frequency of math tutoring this semester 1 = Never 2 = 1–2 times 3 = 3–5 times 4 = 6–10 times 5 = More than 10 times

File Creation

As you create files for analysis, you should document the process for doing so, tracking what files you combined and your decision-making process. If you are doing a multiyear study, a reference table makes it easier to add other files when they become available. Moreover, such a reference document makes it easier for a new staff member to understand the data file creation process.

Suppose you want to look at the influence of services on suspensions and end-of-course exam scores. Your study begins when students are in ninth grade and you create an analytic file for that year. Subsequently, you add tenth-grade data. Table 9 shows a sample data tracking table for a study like this.

Table 9. Sample data tracking table

Program name/ date	Purpose	Input files	Output files	Notes
FixEoC2013 4/28/2014	To combine records from all of the end-of-course exam files	Algebra I 2013 English I 2013 Biology 2013 Civics 2013	AllEoC2013	1 record per student who had taken any end-of-course exam Limit to ninth graders
CrtGrade9 6/14/2014	To compile student records for ninth grade	Membership AllEoC2013 ServicesGrade9	Grade9studentdata	1 record per student linking service data to end-of-course data Keep all students in membership whether or not they participated in services, took exams, or were suspended
FixEoC2014 4/18/2015	To combine records from all end-of-course exam files	Algebra I 2014 English I 2014 Biology 2014 Civics 2014	AllEoC2014	1 record per student who had taken any end-of-course exam Limit to 10th graders
CrtGrade10 6/1/2015	To compile student records for 10th grade	Grade9 StudentData AllEoCGrade10 ServicesGrade10	Grade10studentdata	1 record per student linking service data to end-of-course data Keep all students in Grade9studentdata whether or not they participated in services in 10th grade

The exam scores are tracked by subject, and you want to combine them before linking to the service data. School membership data identify every student in membership at the school at the beginning of ninth grade.

Summary

Keeping track of the data you acquire and create by having an established documentation procedure makes it easier to write reports, collaborate with others, and add additional data to the files.

CHAPTER 4

Data Analysis

Introduction

Once data are defined, collected, and merged, it is time for analysis. There are various ways to do this and you may need to enlist a data analyst, statistician, or educational researcher to assist. A study's design and subsequent analyses can influence the conclusions reached. As an example, consider statistics on graduation rates. By merely varying the denominator in a simple ratio relating the number of graduates to a designated starting enrollment number, you can calculate different graduation rates. If you compare the number of 12th-grade graduates to the size of the same class when students enrolled in 9th grade, the cohort graduation rate (number of graduates divided by number in 9th grade) may be low. If you can only track exits of students within your district and do not know if they transferred to another district, the graduation rate will be lower still. If you compare the number of graduates to the number of incoming 11th-grade students the previous year, the graduation rate will be higher because those who leave school in 9th or 10th grade will not be included. The results depend on how the data are defined, collected, and analyzed.

Analyses can be as simple as setting up a ratio to find a percentage, as in this example. In some cases, averages—mean, median, and mode—may be all you need. Simple spreadsheets (e.g., Excel) can deliver this level of analysis for you. You do not need a trained evaluator to compare parent attendance at a showcase last year and this year and calculate a percentage increase or decrease in attendance. However, if you do not have the requisite training, you should rely on an evaluator or data analyst to run more complex analyses for you. When tasked with monitoring a program, you are responsible for having a general knowledge of analysis language and understanding the strengths and weaknesses of various approaches. For rigorous analysis, your job is just to understand which techniques are appropriate to use and trust your evaluator to do the rest.

When guiding the implementation and progress of a new program, educators often rely on trained evaluators or data analysts to monitor and assess their programs. For that reason, this chapter is not intended to be a primer on data analysis methodologies and statistical tools. Instead, it focuses on awareness and what you need to know about data and data analysis so that you can communicate effectively to all stakeholders.

Choosing Appropriate Analysis Techniques

You have formulated a logic model describing the process through which your program intends to help students. The logic model helps you identify questions to address that can help you improve your program. You have determined the best source for that data and have developed a process for getting it. Once you had the data, you checked its quality and merged files to integrate different kinds of information or to create a longitudinal dataset. You have determined what variables are best to use in the study, modifying existing variables as needed. Now you can begin analyzing the data and getting the answers you need.

The method you use to get those answers depends on the questions you want to address and the data you have available. A descriptive report that focuses on monitoring an intervention does not require a trained evaluator, a comprehensive data system, or statistical software. Analysis questions examine the process by which a program influences outcomes, such as which services are most strongly associated with high school graduation. Evaluation questions result in judgments about the value or the usefulness of something, such as whether students who participated in a program are better prepared for college than those who did not. Addressing these more complex questions requires an evaluation or data analysis background and a more comprehensive student data system. These kinds of analyses may be easier to conduct with a statistical software package.

Analyses can describe services and outcomes, examine the relationships between a given service and a student outcome, or determine whether program participants are better off than students who did not participate in the program. Each type of question provides valuable information about your program.

In evaluating a program, you might design the study to show *evidence of promise or strong evidence of effectiveness*. Evidence of promise means you have empirical evidence showing the link between at least one critical component and at least one relevant outcome in your logic model. It requires a statistically selected comparison group and models that account for other factors that may be associated with outcomes. Strong evidence of effectiveness means the study has a sample size that is large enough to be credible and generalizable and that the design meets the US Department of Education's What Works Clearinghouse standards (What Works Clearinghouse, 2013).

Most data-driven decision efforts at the school or district level do not require using a comparison group. If, however, you are in a position to produce evidence of effectiveness by more rigorous standards, such as those of the What Works Clearinghouse, you can refer to the information in the rest of this chapter regarding comparison groups and analytical techniques. This information is most useful to program evaluators who speak this language and conduct specific analyses.

Strategies for Selecting Comparison Groups

Comparing outcomes for a group of students who received a service or participated in a program (the treatment group) to those who did not receive it (the control group) is essential to determining whether the service or program influenced the outcome. With that in mind, evaluators need to think about defining treatment and comparison groups early so that correct and sufficient data are collected and that reliable analyses can be conducted.

Treatment and control groups should be as similar as possible—*except that the control group did not receive the service.* That is the only way to conclude that outcomes in the treatment group resulted from the service (e.g., tutoring). Numerous factors apart from the service may affect any outcome. An evaluator must define treatment and control groups in a way that accounts for essential differences between the two groups. Regardless of the method used, you should report characteristics of the treatment and control group students to show that the groups are similar. Such characteristics could include race/ethnicity, gender, past academic performance, or poverty status. If students in the treatment and control groups differ, you should present those differences and highlight whether those differences could have influenced results. You can use analytic techniques to account for these differences.

Suppose you want to know whether math tutoring influenced math test scores. If the treatment group students take Algebra I and the control group students take Geometry, then the course they were taking might influence their test scores. Likewise, if the treatment group has few students eligible for free lunch while the control group has many, family income may influence test scores. The treatment and control groups should be as similar as possible on measures that may influence their academic outcomes, and in this example, they are not. Defining groups through random assignment or propensity score matching (described later in this section) is required to show evidence of promise or strong evidence of effectiveness.

Comparing Pre- and Post-test Scores

Comparing student performance before and after receiving a service is one way to consider whether a service made a difference over time. However, that set of students who had not yet received services does not constitute a control group. The post-service students are exactly the same as the pre-service students, but you cannot attribute their gains in math scores to the tutoring alone. Suppose the math tutoring program lasted one semester. Students took exams at the beginning and then the end of the semester, and their scores improved. Over the course of the semester, these students would have learned more math—even without tutoring—and their scores should have improved. Thus, to understand whether tutoring influenced these gains requires comparing their gains to those of students with similar characteristics who took the same math class but did not receive tutoring.

Selection into the Service

Similarly, evaluators need to account for the process by which students are selected to receive the service. Students may have volunteered for the tutoring, parents may have enrolled the students in the tutoring, or teachers may have nominated select students to take the tutoring. Allowing individuals to choose a service leads to biased results because those who choose to participate may differ from those who do not. Perhaps children who volunteer for math tutoring have greater interest or more ability to do well in math than those who do not, and this interest or ability leads to higher math scores. Perhaps parents who enroll their children in tutoring are more involved with their children's school activities, and this involvement causes scores to improve. Perhaps teachers nominate students based on ability, motivation, or persistence, all of which could be associated with higher math scores. Several approaches to avoid introducing this sort of selection bias are discussed in the following sections.

Longitudinal Panel Design

Particularly with a whole-school reform model, you can compare the cohort of students who first received services (cohort A) to the cohort immediately before the reform was implemented (cohort B). With a whole-school reform model, all of cohort A students are eligible for the program, whereas none of cohort B students would have participated. Characteristics of students in one school do not change much from one year to the next, and school resources and teaching staff may not change much from one year to the next. In this case, the cohort A students are like the cohort B students—except that they are part of the whole-school reform.

These assumptions may not always be correct. Students may differ from one cohort to the next in ways that are associated with key outcomes of interest. Whole-school reform can change the student body if students from other schools apply to get in or if students who would have attended leave. Even if the characteristics of the student body do not change from one year to the next, you want to learn about the services available to students in the year before the reform was implemented. The school reform model may include tutoring for all students, but in the year before, tutoring may have been available for some students.

Other Nonstatistical Approaches to Matching

You can match treatment and control students based on various student characteristics. For example, a student in the treatment group who is female, has limited English proficiency, and scored below grade level in math can be matched to another student with those characteristics. This approach does not use a probabilistic technique, but it does ensure that students in each group match on these characteristics so that the groups are similar.

Random Assignment

Ideally, students are randomly assigned to treatment or control groups. Under this method, students are selected into the service by a chance factor, such as tossing a coin. With random assignment, no characteristic of a child would influence his or her receiving the treatment. Suppose that the tutoring service is voluntary, and eligible students choose to take it. If so, you need to randomly assign from the group of students who have expressed interest in the tutoring. You can ask students to apply to the service and confirm that they are able to enroll. Then, you randomly assign from that eligible list to the treatment or control group. If you try to randomly assign students to the treatment using the list of all students, many of them may choose not to participate because they are not interested or because the timing does not fit their schedule. This kind of opting out means that the treatment group and the control group are not similar. So, random assignment must occur *after* the pool of students has been confirmed, not before.

For most student service providers, denying services to a group of students who express interest may seem unfair. To compensate, strategies to help the control group students include offering different kinds of services to students in each group, where the treatment group receives more intense services than the control group. For example, the control group might receive a 4-week service while the treatment group receives a 16-week service. Alternatively, you might stagger the timing of the service so that control-group students receive it after the evaluation is complete (e.g., the following semester).

Propensity Score Matching

Random assignment may not be possible because you had difficulties in assigning students or you are analyzing retrospective data. Propensity score matching is a statistical technique used to create two groups of matched students. Propensity score matching creates a comparison group by estimating which individuals have a high probability (or propensity) of being part of the treatment group based on observed characteristics. The comparison group is created by matching students who receive the treatment with similar students who do not based on observable attributes. Propensity score matching requires a large sample size, and it cannot account for unobserved characteristics that may be associated with selection into the treatment group. For example, the school may not have data about students' motivation. Yet, this technique does reduce bias compared to other methods.

Choosing an Analytic Technique

Depending on the questions you want to answer, the type of data you have, and the resources you can dedicate to a study, you can choose from different analytic techniques. Here we describe a few techniques that address different kinds of questions. Descriptive analyses focus on one variable without testing for statistical significance. Techniques such as correlations, t-tests, and analysis of variance (ANOVA) examine the relationships between two variables and test the statistical significance of those relationships. Multiple regression strategies allow simultaneous examination of multiple factors associated with an outcome.

Statistical significance expresses the possibility that a given outcome could have occurred just by chance. Evaluators often use a probability level of 5 percent or less as an indicator that a result is statistically significant. That means that in replicating the study, you would expect the outcome to occur by chance only 5 percent of the time. Thus, 95 percent of the time, you can assume the outcome would occur because of a meaningful association between the variables.

Descriptive Analysis

Monitoring the program means tracking and describing whether the program is being implemented as it ought to be and whether it is meeting its designated targets. Here, you can use strategies such as calculating percentages, frequencies, averages, and ranges. To find out what percentage of 11th grade students participated in a college visit, you can track the total number of 11th graders, the number of them who participated in a college visit and then calculate the percentage of 11th grade students who participated. To examine performance on the end-of-course Algebra I exam, you can calculate the average test score, or you can identify the percentage of students who passed. If you want to learn about changes in use of parental services over time, you can calculate a percentage increase or decrease in the number of parents participating in activities.

When conducting descriptive analyses, you should look at the distribution of the data to make sure you use the best method. For example, when you want to compare groups of different sizes, you should calculate a percentage rather than simply reporting numbers. You might find that in high school A, 50 juniors participated in the college visit compared with 75 juniors in school B. A difference of 25 students seems big—unless you know that school A has 100 juniors and school B has 150 juniors. Then the rates of participation are exactly the same. Similarly, when calculating averages, such as the average test score, you should consider whether the mean or the median is more appropriate. The mean is the mathematical average, whereas the median is the central value. If one record has a value much different from the others, the mean could be misleading. Consider exam scores for five students who received tutoring: 90, 85, 95, 88, and 40. Here, one student had a far lower score than the others—perhaps she was not feeling well or had a troubling experience at home. The mean is $(90 + 85 + 95 + 88 + 40) / 5 = 80$. The median involves putting the scores in rank order and selecting the middle one: 40, 85, 88, 90, and 95. The median is 88, which better represents this group's overall performance.

Descriptive analyses serve to monitor whether the program is working as intended. They do not test for statistical significance and they do not permit making causal claims about the program. Because you do not need linked student-level data or a comparison group, and you can use spreadsheets to do these calculations and can conduct these analyses for the duration of the program.

Correlation

A correlation analysis focuses on the relationship between two variables. It might be used to assess a question such as, "Are more hours of tutoring associated with a higher grade point average?" This method does not compare results from one group to another, but rather examines the strength of the relationship for all members of a single group. When two measures are correlated, variation in one corresponds to variation in the other. Correlation coefficients range from -1 to 1, with -1 and 1 indicating perfect correlations and 0 indicating no association at all. The closer the coefficient is to the absolute value of 1, the stronger the association.

If tutoring hours and GPA are positively correlated, then you expect to see higher GPAs among students who had more tutoring hours. When measures increase or decrease together, you have a positive correlation. Some measures are negatively correlated, and an increase in one is associated with a decrease in the other. For example, you expect unexcused absences and GPA to be negatively correlated. As the number of missed school days increases, the GPA decreases.

Correlation analyses in program evaluations never yield perfect correlations with a value of 1 or -1. For example, you would not expect that for every 20 hours spent in tutoring, the GPA increases exactly 0.1 for every student. You cannot perfectly predict a student's GPA by knowing the hours spent in tutoring. However, you can get a sense of the strength of the association between tutoring and GPA and use that information accordingly.

Finding a weak association between hours of tutoring and GPA suggests that the tutoring program does not influence GPA very much. Perhaps the tutoring services need to be modified. Perhaps hours of tutoring are associated with performance in a specific subject, which does not dramatically affect the overall GPA. Examining the correlation between hours of tutoring and grades in the associated subject can highlight that specific relationship.

What if the correlation between hours of tutoring and GPA is strong? Does that prove that tutoring causes GPAs to increase? Correlation does not indicate causation. Finding a strong correlation suggests that tutoring hours may influence GPA, but other factors may have an influence too. Perhaps students with many tutoring hours are more motivated and have higher aspirations for educational attainment, and their motivation and aspirations influence their GPA. Perhaps those with many tutoring hours also participate extensively in mentoring services, in which they gain affective supports that influence their GPA beyond the tutoring. Other kinds of analyses permit exploring this kind of question.

The t-Test

The t-test is used to examine the differences in averages between two independent groups or two subgroups. You can use a t-test to address the question, "Do students who participate in our program get better Algebra I grades than students who do not?" The t-test can only have two mutually exclusive groups—that is, members of one group cannot be included in the other group. For this question, students are either in the program or not, and you must have a data on a well-defined comparison group. A statistically significant finding that participating students had better Algebra I grades than their peers suggests that your program is helping these students improve in Algebra I.

The t-test can also be used to measure the differences in averages between subgroups of students within your program. For example, the question, "Do first-generation college-goers do as well in Algebra I as students whose parents went to college?" compares students who are first-generation college-goers (i.e., neither parent has more than a high school diploma) to students whose parents have at least some college. Here, all students participate in your program, and analyses control for program participation. Finding no statistically significant difference between the scores of the first-generation college-goers and their peers suggests that students are doing equally well, regardless of their parents' educational attainment. However, finding that first-generation college-goers have lower scores than their peers suggests these students are not doing as well, even with your program services. With this information, you might decide to target additional services to first-generation college-goers. You can also examine other factors that may influence algebra scores. If the Pre-algebra scores of first-generation college-goers are lower than those of their peers, you might decide to focus targeted services on Pre-algebra. Reducing differences in Pre-algebra performance might reduce differences in performance in subsequent mathematics classes.

ANOVA

The t-test is appropriate for the question about subgroups of students because it has only two subgroups: first-generation college-goers and those whose parents went to college. The second t-test question compares the two-category program participation measure. If you have more than two categories, however, ANOVA is better for testing differences in means.

Suppose your students are white, Hispanic, African American, and Native American, and you want to look at the association between race/ethnicity and performance in Algebra I. Conducting multiple t-tests to compare each population against the others can quickly become complicated. Instead, you can conduct an ANOVA to look at the overall association between race/ethnicity and Algebra I performance.

As with the t-test, ANOVA requires that groups are independent of each other—students can be included in only one group. A statistically significant ANOVA result tells you that at least two of the groups differ, but not which groups differ from each other.

Chi-Square Test

The chi-square test permits testing relationships between two categorical variables, showing whether they are independent of each other. If you can cross-tabulate two variables, the chi-square test determines what you would expect to see if the two variables are independent of each other. If the variables are independent, then the service has no influence on the outcome. You expect the distribution of responses to be about the same between the service participants and nonparticipants. The chi-square test compares the actual results to the expected results to indicate whether the two variables are independent of each other. If the actual results differ greatly from the expected results, then you can conclude that variables are associated. For example, you can link information about parental participation in meetings about paying for college and their perceptions of college affordability using a chi-square test to see whether participation in the meetings is associated with perceptions. If the distribution of perceptions of college affordability is the same for participants and nonparticipants, you can conclude that the meetings are not working as intended. Perhaps you can rethink the way you provide information in those meetings. You may want to develop new materials for these meetings or you may want to try a different delivery system.

Note that chi-square tests and correlations are sensitive to sample size. With large samples, even small differences may appear statistically significant. Chi-square tests are also sensitive to the small distributions within cells. Before doing a chi-square test, you should look at the frequencies in the cells of the table. If you have cells with very few respondents (say, fewer than five cases), you can combine categories to increase the numbers within each cell. Your question about whether a parent thought college was affordable might have five categories (definitely, possibly, not sure, probably not, definitely not). If the cross-tabulation shows that there are small cell sizes, you can create a three-category variable by combining "definitely" with "possibly" and "probably not" with "definitely not." If only one or two people say "not sure," you can omit that category rather than combining it with the others.

Multiple Linear Regression

Multiple factors influence any given outcome, and multiple linear regression is a statistical way to examine the relationship among various explanatory factors and an outcome. Multiple linear regression is used to assess a question such as, "Did participation in my program influence Algebra I scores after accounting for past math performance and aspirations?" The explanatory factors are your program, each student's past math performance, and each student's aspirations. The outcome is the Algebra I score.

Addressing the question this way acknowledges that in addition to benefits from program participation, factors such as performance in past math classes and aspirations could influence Algebra I scores. A student who did well in prior math classes may have an easier time meeting challenges in Algebra I. Students who plan to go to college may put more effort into their studies than students who do not. Regression analysis permits examining those factors simultaneously to see whether the service in question influences the outcome beyond those other factors. Here, you can think of regression as constructing a formula for the math score that includes variables that may provide alternate explanations for Algebra I scores. Correlations and t-tests may help determine which measures to include. For example, finding that aspirations are correlated with mathematics performance suggests you should include aspirations in the analysis. As with other analyses, appropriate data are necessary. Answering this sample question requires having data about each student's prior math performance and having survey data in which students reported their aspirations.

Analysis results might indicate that the relationship between program participation and the student's Algebra I score is statistically significant, even when you control for the other factors. Accounting for other explanatory factors increases confidence in the conclusion that your program influences Algebra I scores. However, this result does not necessarily mean that the program caused the improved Algebra I score. Perhaps other factors that you could not include in the analysis contributed to the outcome. Even so, this result does show an association between program participation and the outcome.

Alternatively, this multiple regression analysis might indicate that once prior achievement is included in the model, the effect of participation in your program on Algebra I scores dissipates. In other words, students' prior achievement might be the strongest predictor of Algebra I scores. This result suggests the need to target additional resources to students who have struggled with math. Perhaps students who have not performed well in middle school mathematics need a bridge program or other supports to help them succeed in Algebra I. By understanding the way different factors are associated with each other, you can develop or refine services to better meet student needs.

Logistic Regression

In multiple linear regression (described above), the outcome variables (Algebra I score) must be an interval or ratio, which means that differences between the levels of the variable are equal (as discussed in Chapter 3). Here, it makes sense to say an Algebra I score of 282 is two more than a score of 280, and a score of 270 is 5 less than a score of 275. Examining a yes/no outcome, such as high school dropout and college enrollment, requires a different approach. Here, logistic regression models are appropriate.

If you wanted to examine the question, "Did participation in my program influence college enrollment after accounting for past math performance and aspirations?" you would have a yes/no outcome. A logistic regression model yields the odds of college enrollment given program participation, even when accounting for other factors that might predict the outcome, such as prior math performance and aspirations. Results might indicate, for example, that participants were two times more likely to enroll in college than those who did not participate in the program, even when prior math performance and aspirations are included in the model.

As with the multiple linear regression example, you may find that including additional measures reduces the association between your program and the outcome. That information can highlight services you may want to expand or modify.

Summary

Data analyses can be resource intensive, particularly if you are acquiring, linking, analyzing, and reporting on new data. In deciding which methods to use, you need to be strategic in deciding how the project can benefit from the new information. Those involved with the program have the best insights about which kinds of additional knowledge can yield the greatest benefit. For example, it may be of the greatest importance to determine which services are most influential for a given outcome. Alternatively, when introducing an innovative program that departs from past practices, it may be most important to quickly obtain information that would help you modify it if needed. Regardless of whether the goal is to monitor a program or conduct an evaluation, it is crucial to have accurate data and use appropriate methods to guide your decision-making efforts.

If your study has a control group, you must ensure that the treatment and control groups are as similar as possible, except that students in the control group do not receive the service. With careful consideration in defining treatment and control groups, you are better able to understand the potential influence of a service on student outcomes.

Descriptive analyses allow researchers to examine program implementation. Techniques uch as correlations, t-tests, and ANOVA permit identifying a relationship between two items. On their own, these approaches do not meet criteria for evidence of promise or strong evidence of effectiveness. However, they are methods for conducting statistical hypothesis tests, which help identify key relationships between service recipients and outcomes. Multiple regression permits incorporating different factors to isolate the influence of the program on outcomes.

CHAPTER 5

Dissemination

Introduction

Dissemination is often mistaken for the distribution of information, similar to a newspaper on your front porch, but it is much more complex than printing a handout or designing a flyer. Engaging in dissemination implies that you have information to share, but it also implies that you need to be clear about your audience, the intended outcomes for various audiences, and the specific needs of various audiences (not like a newspaper on your front porch!).

In some cases, your sole purpose is to increase the knowledge of your audience. If the school board has changed the attendance boundaries in your district, a principal may have to share this information with parents (as opposed to seeking their input) to explain a new bus schedule. In this case, the spotlight is on the principal, not on the parents. Little is expected of the parents as this information is provided.

At other times, your purpose may be to change individual practice at the classroom level or establish system-wide change. In this case, your dissemination efforts may include skill building as well as information sharing. Consider the "flipped" classroom in which students learn new information outside of school hours and complete exercises with the teacher during class. Providing a definition and a list of expected benefits will not result in new classroom practices. Teachers need training that includes examples of best practices and time to try out a new skill set to give them a chance at succeeding with a flipped classroom. Dissemination practices that are aimed at changing practice or influencing a system require the audience to relate the new information and skills to current knowledge and practice, integrate and organize the new skills in ways that are practical, and monitor their own change and understanding throughout the process (Hutchinson & Huberman, 1993).

This approach to dissemination opens up the process to a focus on the role of the recipient, a fairly new idea. The older approach to dissemination emphasized, almost exclusively, the role of the information provider with a "build it and they will come" attitude. Providers shared information with little thought or concern about the end user. The work of Ely and Huberman (1993) initiated a shift in thinking about dissemination and provides a broader expectation for the dissemination of information. The authors observe that the purpose of communicating information to specific audiences is extending knowledge with a view to modifying policies and practices if necessary.

More simply put, dissemination is the transfer of knowledge *with the expectation that it will be used*. With this added emphasis, Ely and Huberman's (1993) *User-Friendly Handbook* became the primer for dissemination plans. The authors provide a new way of thinking, one that promotes adaptation and long-term implementation and recognizes end users as principal players in the process. They discuss four levels of effort—spread, choice, exchange, and implementation—and the related commitments of disseminators and users (Dissemination Analysis Group in Herlig, 1977).

> **Spread**—a one-way casting out of knowledge in all its forms—requires much of the provider and little of the receiver. It is a proactive initiative in which information is scattered randomly via print, video (e.g., YouTube), or audio; at meetings; online (anything from professional webinars to Facebook); in journals or newspapers; or via e-mail. The onus is on the provider to prepare the information, and no responsibility is placed on the receiver.
>
> **Choice**—actively helping users seek information and learn about options—differs from spread in that information is sought by the user. As a dissemination strategy, it is dependent on the users' awareness that information exists that might interest them. Choice requires that disseminators strategically place information in places that potential users might look for it, for example, in online discussion boards or via toll-free telephone numbers. There are no face-to-face encounters in the choice mode of dissemination.
>
> **Exchange**—a two-way flow of information involving interactions between people—is an interactive process that implies that potential users are interested enough in the information to interact with providers, share information (perhaps participate in a needs assessment), ask questions, and voice concerns. As a dissemination strategy, exchange is most effective in face-to-face settings where both disseminators

and users are willing participants. This can occur in professional development sessions, workshops, webinars, and conferences.

Implementation—using new information with training, assistance, and support—is the ultimate goal of most dissemination efforts that involve placing new programs in schools and enhancing classroom practices. At this point, emphasis shifts to the user whose practice is adapting to new information and new expectations, while at the same time remaining dependent on support and encouragement along the way. Interaction in a safe and trusting environment between the user and provider fosters successful implementation of new programs and skills.

The remaining sections of this chapter address the types of dissemination decisions that most project or program directors, school administrators, researchers, and professional developers face at some point.

Understanding and Supporting Your Audience

Projects, whether they are bake sales or major school-wide operational changes, have one thing in common: the project leaders will at some point be required to share information—before, during, or after the project—with a variety of interested people. School boards need to prepare the community for the building of a new high school and adjusting student attendance zones. Principals need to prepare their staffs when switching from traditional to block scheduling, but teachers need different information and support than do parents and students. In other words, a message may wear many hats as it is tailored for various audiences (University of North Carolina at Chapel Hill, n.d.).

Leaders tasked with implementing new ideas wear the mantle of "change agent." Whatever the focus of the new program, the format of the new schedule, or the changes in the cafeteria menu, the fact remains that it represents a change—a change from what used to be. Keeping in mind that change is not welcomed by everyone, change agents—project directors, principals, school boards—must decide how to deliver their message and generate buy-in from their audience. Do not assume that your reader or listener knows about the subject. For example, a quick reference to "the GEAR UP program" or "early college high school" without explaining the term may leave an audience of parents or policy makers stymied and resistant. Change agents must also remember that "possession of information does not mean it will be used" (Newman & Vash, 1994, p. 381).

Keep in mind that every audience wants something from you. The obvious need of each audience is information, and your task is to determine what information they need (what is most important to them and what is not), how they will best understand the information, and what they will do with it. Various audiences need and use information differently. If you are announcing a fait accompli (e.g., the date is set for the bake sale), the expectation for the audience is awareness and acceptance. If, however, you hope to implement a new elementary reading program, your hope for the audience is understanding and some level of use or commitment.

Suppose that your district is implementing a dual-enrollment program at the area high schools. The plan is to partner with the local community college and let seniors enroll in designated English and history courses in the fall and spring semesters, thus earning 12 college credits by the time they graduate from high school. The college courses will replace their required high school English and history classes, but students will receive high school credit (Carnegie units) upon successful completion of their college counterpart. You are tasked with recruiting the students for the program, seeking support from principals and teachers, providing status updates to school administrators, communicating with the community college instructors, and monitoring student progress and program implementation. These responsibilities cast you as a change agent and require you to devise multiple approaches to disseminating program information to your various stakeholders. The following sections describe dissemination strategies about dual enrollment for different audiences.

Students and Parents

In recruiting students and parents for the dual-enrollment program, your main focus is on providing clear and accurate information about the program to encourage student enrollment. As a disseminator, your approach is one of *spread*—the heaviest responsibility lies with you. You must work to prepare information in such a way that it is convincing, persuasive, and transparent. There is an element of *exchange* in this scenario if the dissemination plan includes face-to-face meetings (as opposed to announcements via e-mail or newspaper) where students and parents can ask questions, express concerns, and seek advice. The expected use of the information you disseminate is that the students and parents make the best decision for themselves (Table 10).

Table 10. Disseminating dual-enrollment information to students and parents

What information is needed	Benefits of program, meaning of dual credits, enrollment at the community college, location of classes, impact on high school schedule, point of contact
How to foster understanding	Spread: mass letter or e-mail effort
	Exchange: face-to-face presentation with Q&A session
Anticipated use of information	Enrollment in the program
Interaction with disseminator	Minimal; available as source of information

Administrators

As the program commences, the high school principals and central office staff require periodic reports on program implementation—successes and challenges. This is most often a written report, stating facts about enrollment, attendance, grades, and so on. You can include tables and graphs accompanied by clear and concise text to focus attention on the points you wish to emphasize. Administrators need the information to assess the value and benefits of the program, review any unexpected hurdles, and make decisions about the life expectancy of the program. This is considered a *targeted spread* because the audience is limited and little is required of the end user (Table 11).

Table 11. Disseminating dual-enrollment information to administrators

What information is needed	Factual academic, enrollment, and participation information; procedural issues
How to foster understanding	Spread: report, primarily focused on quantitative data
Anticipated use of information	Decision making
Interaction with disseminator	Minimal; available as source of information

Funders/Policy Makers

In the dual-enrollment example, the school board is the funder and policy maker. In addition to copies of the written reports submitted to local administrators, the board may request a presentation at a school board meeting. If so, this dissemination involves the *exchange* of information. Board members may have questions about issues not covered in the report, and, like the administrators, they need the information provided to determine future support for the program and other similar endeavors. For funders like the National Science Foundation and the US Department of Education and for policy makers in Congress, program directors submit reports presenting evidence of success and support for continued funding. Federal funders require rigorous evidence of program success, and, if your program evaluator has conducted a quasi-experimental study or a randomized controlled trial, the results will be of interest to this audience (Table 12).

Table 12. Disseminating dual-enrollment information to funders and policy makers

What information is needed	Factual academic, enrollment, and participation information; procedural issues; partnerships
How to foster understanding	Spread: report, primarily focused on quantitative data
	Exchange: presentation
Anticipated use of information	Decision making
Interaction with disseminator	Q&A session during presentation of report/findings

Program Staff

In dual-enrollment efforts, program staff include the program director and the community college instructors assigned to the program. It is your responsibility to ensure that the instructors are trained to make the transition to teaching high school seniors, especially if the courses are conducted on the high school campus. They need to adjust to normal school operational protocols, align the high school syllabi to the community college syllabi, and understand their responsibility in contributing to the final high school transcripts of the enrolled students. Your dissemination approach must be one of *implementation*—ensuring an interactive relationship with the program staff that includes routine support and technical assistance. If you are the project director for a new school-wide program such as block scheduling, your dissemination efforts with program staff represent a more rigorous example of implementation. As project director, you are responsible for the professional development of classroom teachers, school liaisons, coaches, and various support players. New programs require new skills for successful translation into new classroom practices, and this suggests ongoing training and technical assistance for all involved (Table 13).

Table 13. Disseminating dual-enrollment information to program staff

What information is needed	New skills, classroom practices; student needs; grading procedures; general technical assistance
How to foster understanding	Exchange: regular meetings
	Implementation: ongoing support, assistance
Anticipated use of information	Program improvement
Interaction with disseminator	High and frequent

To further emphasize the importance of understanding how your audience can use the information you provide (disseminate), consider an example from Machlup (1993), who asks:

Does *use of information*—the process of transmission and reception, for example, of a letter—mean (1) receiving it and thus getting a chance to read it; (2) receiving and actually reading it; (3) receiving, reading, and understanding it; (4) receiving, reading, understanding, and appreciating it; (5) receiving, reading, understanding, appreciating, and making it the basis of a decision; or (6) receiving, reading, understanding, and appreciating it, plus letting it help you in making a decision and taking an action (or refusing to act) in line with the decision reached with the help of the knowledge obtained? (pp. 449–450)

The question illustrates the many interpretations of the word *dissemination* and how its casual use can lead to unintended results. If Machlup's hypothetical letter is an announcement of a new program you are introducing to your school district that seeks to recruit teachers who are willing to participate, the steps would align as illustrated in Table 14.

Table 14. Use of information comparisons: hypothetical versus actual

Machlup levels	School example
Receiving	Recipients receive the announcement
Receiving and reading	Recipients open and read the announcement
Receiving, reading, and understanding	Recipients understand the opportunity to participate
Receiving, reading, understanding, and appreciating	Recipients appreciate being included in the announcement
Receiving, reading, understanding, appreciating, and deciding (Y or N)	Recipients make a decision about participating
Taking or not taking action based on previous steps	Recipients take visible action (this is the only step that can be documented by disseminators)

In this example, the unintended result for you is that you have no evidence of the information being used until the last step. Even at that point, if the decision is made not to take action, you only have indirect proof of the use of the information. This example points out the inherent shortcoming of *spread* as a reliable dissemination strategy when you need a response from the intended users. Examples of other tactics related to the four major goals of dissemination include those listed in Table 15.

Table 15. Common dissemination strategies

Audience	Common dissemination strategies			
	Spread	Choice	Exchange	Implementation
Students/parents	Mass letter or e-mail effort	Program website	PTA meeting Personal e-mail	
Program staff	Recruitment announcement	Professional literature	Staff meetings Conferences	Technical assistance
Administrators	Project reports	Findings from similar programs	Presentation	
Policy makers/funders	Project reports		Presentation	
Researchers		Targeted journals	Presentation/ panel discussion	

The closing message is: disseminator, beware. Widen the scope of your dissemination efforts beyond the overused spread mode. A spread approach—flyers, newspaper articles—is often the first step of a longer dissemination journey, one that can lead you through choice, exchange, and implementation. This is a progression that requires you to know your role in each phase and the anticipated role of the end users. It requires a commitment of time, energy, and funding.

Disseminating Findings through Various Media

As your project progresses and when it draws to a close, you may be encouraged by your funder to share project findings within your community and with other education stakeholders. Whether preparing for conference presentations or publications, there are some overarching recommendations to keep in mind as you decide how to share project outcomes and lessons learned. Although this section focuses on preparing manuscripts as a means of dissemination, these recommendations also can apply to presentations.

Selecting Your Medium

The audience for whom you are preparing your information often dictates the most suitable medium for presenting your findings (Education Development Center, n.d.). You may also find yourself preparing multiple versions of your findings for various audiences, such as local constituents, funding agents, or academic researchers. Over the course of your project, you may be expected to write an article for your school, district, or state newsletter or even for the local newspaper; prepare a presentation for the PTA or school board; submit a progress report for a funding agent; or develop a technical and academic paper for an educational journal. Most likely, you may be asked to do some version of all of the above, which means working with the same information but varying the language and the points of emphasis to accommodate the interests of various readers and listeners.

Typically, local stakeholders are most interested in local results—where were you before the project and where are you now? What got you here? How can future improvements be ensured? How have your students and teachers benefitted from the new program? Whether preparing to answer these questions in print or in a presentation, you should keep your language simple, your findings clear, and your emphasis on progress.

Funders are the agents or agencies providing the financial support for a project, and most place an emphasis on facts. They may ask for the technical information put forth in your grant—what activities are you offering, and how many students/parents are attending? Funders often have their own reporting forms and processes for you to follow. The annual performance review that GEAR UP grantees submit to the US Department of Education is an example.

Practitioners and researchers tend to be interested in the quality and replicability of your findings—what were the research questions, what was the data source, and how were the data collected and analyzed? Researchers are most interested in your analysis design and methodology. If you want to publish your findings in an educational journal, it is up to you to identify the appropriate journal. Check the authors' guidelines that are provided by most journals for specific requirements.

Keep in mind that across the life of a project, you may be required to prepare findings for numerous different audiences in various formats, and it is up to you to tailor the content to meet the needs of each audience. So, knowing the audience is essential and just as important as understanding the medium.

Organizing the Content

Framing the structure of a manuscript or presentation organizes your thoughts as well as the materials you plan to include in the discussion. Your high school English teacher was right—an outline really does help! Consider the contents of key sections such as the introduction, methods, results, discussion, and conclusion:

Introduction. Readers need to know what you are studying and why it is important. This section provides the context for the study and usually describes the program's students and academic conditions. It is a good place to include the project's logic model and state the general research question or questions.

Methods. This section describes the analysis plan, data collection instruments, and analysis methods. It also confirms the reliability and validity of methods used. If you are preparing a manuscript for publication or a report for a funder, this will be the technical section in which you describe your analysis tools such t-tests, chi-squares, or ANOVAs. A presentation for local stakeholders will omit many of these more technical aspects in favor of reporting results.

Results. The results section provides a factual presentation of the analysis results and is supported with appropriate tables or graphs. Again, the audience caveat applies. Readers of a research journal appreciate more sophisticated visual representations and explanations than a local audience.

Discussion. In the discussion section, you provide an interpretation of the results you presented in the previous section. You should also address limitations and, to the extent possible, relate the discussion to the information provided in the introduction.

Conclusion. In the conclusion, you discuss what was learned, as related to the purpose of the study and the general research questions. Decision makers look for recommendations based on the analysis of the data collected.

Although this list may vary in different media (for example, it may be helpful to include an executive summary or an abstract for a research journal), it represents what your audience expects in a well-developed paper or presentation.

Presenting Your Data: More about Methods and Results

Readers are interested in the data—what was collected, how it was collected, and why it was analyzed using a particular method. Relating data to a research question or a local situation (e.g., low graduation rates, low mathematics achievement) justifies your choices about what data were most important in the data collection effort. Readers and listeners want to know where the data were acquired or how they were collected. For example, did you access existing school records, state or national databases, or SLDSs? Did you create your own data collection instruments? Did you collect student-level data? How are the data that you collected related to the decisions you need to make?

All results presented visually—tables and graphs—should be supported with text explanations in the body of the paper. The text should provide a thoughtful interpretation for the data in the table, not merely duplicate it in narrative form. Choose wisely. The reader should not have to make meaning out of the tables or graphs included in the paper but should find clear, concise interpretations of the data presented. An example of clear, supporting text for Figure 5 would be, *"Ninth-grade end-of-grade math scores at East High are noticeably higher than at the other three area high schools, but all four schools show similar low scores in English."*

Figure 5. Example of text-to-table relationship

a. Example of figure

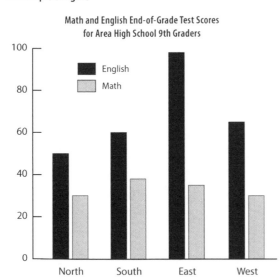

Math and English End-of-Grade Test Scores
for Area High School 9th Graders

■ English
▨ Math

North   South   East   West

b. Example of Supporting Text

Ninth-grade end-of-grade math scores at East High are noticeably higher than at the other three area high schools—about 90 percent versus 50 percent to 62 percent. However, all four schools show similar low scores in English—30 percent to 39 percent.

Postscript

Even the most competent writers and experienced presenters adhere to the
following advice:

- Cite your references.

- Edit your submission: spell-check and proof-read.

- Check fonts and spacing: cutting and pasting can introduce unsightly
  mistakes.

- Avoid formatting errors: journal editors and reviewers will not read
  sloppy work.

- Follow journal or funder guidelines for submission: guidelines differ, so
  ignore at your peril.

Final Thoughts

As you share information about your project, you should consider the
following questions: what is your dissemination goal, who is your audience,
what does your audience really need to know, how will they use the
information, what interactions between disseminator and potential user
are necessary, and what media are best for your intended dissemination?
Well-planned dissemination activities guide your audience through your
data-driven decision-making process, generate confidence in your data-
driven decisions, and provide transparency that leads to ongoing support for
and understanding of the process. Dissemination is a strong and valuable
communication tool that allows you to involve and inform your colleagues
and make data-driven decision making a collaborative endeavor. Use it to your
advantage.

References

Achieve, Inc. (2009). *Race to the Top: Accelerating college and career readiness – Standards and assessments.* Washington, DC. Retrieved from http://www. achieve.org/files/RTTT-StandardsandAssessments.pdf

Attewell, P., Lavin, D., Domina, T., & Levey, T. (2006). New evidence on college remediation. *The Journal of Higher Education, 77*(5), 886–924.

Bennett, C. (1975, March/April). Up the hierarchy. *Journal of Extension, 13*(2), 7–12.

Bernhardt, V. (1998). *Data analysis for comprehensive schoolwide improvement.* Larchmont, NY: Eye on Education.

Conley, D. T. (2008). What makes a student college ready? *Educational Leadership, 66*(2). Retrieved from http://www.ascd.org/publications/ educational-leadership/oct08/vol66/num02/What-Makes-a-Student-College-Ready%C2%A2.aspx

Couper, M. P. (2008). *Designing effective web surveys.* New York, NY: Cambridge University Press.

Data Quality Campaign. (2006). *Creating a longitudinal data system: Using data to improve student achievement.* Washington, DC. Retrieved from http://www.dataqualitycampaign.org/files/109_Publications-Creating_Longitudinal_Data_System.pdf

Data Quality Campaign. (2011). *State analysis by essential element.* Washington, DC. Retrieved from http://www.dataqualitycampaign.org/ your-states-progress/10-essential-elements/

Data Quality Campaign. (2013). *Data for action 2013.* Washington, DC. Retrieved from http://www.dataqualitycampaign.org/files/ DataForAction2013.pdf

Data Quality Campaign. (2015). *State analysis by state action.* Washington, DC. Retrieved from http://www.dataqualitycampaign.org/your-states-progress/10-state-actions/

Dillman, D. A., Smyth, J. D., & Christian, L. M. (2008). *Internet, mail, and mixed-mode surveys: The tailored design method* (3rd ed.). Hoboken, NJ: John Wiley & Sons, Inc.

Dynarski, S. M., Hemelt, S. W., & Hyman, J. M. (2015). The missing manual: Using National Student Clearinghouse data to track postsecondary outcomes. *Educational Evaluation and Policy Analysis, 37*(1S), 53S–79S.

Education Development Center. (n.d.). *Resources for teacher leadership: Writing for publication*. Retrieved from http://teacherleadership.edc.org/writingforpub.asp

Ely, D., & Huberman, A. M. (1993). *User-friendly handbook for project dissemination: Science, mathematics, engineering, and technology education.* Washington, DC: The National Science Foundation.

Engel, R., & Schutt, R. (2013). Chapter 4: Measurement. In R. Engel & R. Schutt (Eds.), *The practice of research in social work* (3rd ed.). Thousand Oaks, CA: Sage Publications. Retrieved from http://www.sagepub.com/upm-data/45955_chapter_4.pdf

Herlig, R. (1977). *The tenth annual dissemination conference: A report.* Washington, DC: Council of Chief State School Officers. Retrieved from http://files.eric.ed.gov/fulltext/ED146939.pdf

Hutchinson, J., & Huberman, A. M. (1993). *Knowledge dissemination and use in science and mathematics education: A literature review.* Washington, DC: The National Science Foundation.

Kellogg Foundation. (2004). *Using logic models to bring together planning, evaluation, and action: Logic model development guide.* Battle Creek, MI: Kellogg Foundation.

Klein, S. S., & Gwaltney, M. K. (1991, March). Charting the education dissemination system. *Science Communication, 12*(3), 241–265.

Machlup, F. (1993, June). Uses, value, and benefits of knowledge. *Science Communication, 14*(4), 448–466.

McCallister, E., Grance, T., & Scarfon, K. (2010). *Guide to protecting the confidentiality of personally identifiable information (PII).* (National Institute of Standards and Technology, Special Publication 800-122). Washington, DC: US Department of Commerce.

National Center for Education Statistics. (2011). *The condition of education 2011* (NCES 2011-033). Washington, DC: National Center for Education Statistics, Institute of Education Sciences, US Department of Education.

National Student Clearinghouse. (n.d.). *StudentTracker for outreach* [Data file]. Retrieved from http://www.studentclearinghouse.org/outreach/

Newman, S., & Vash, C. (1994). Gray matter: Utilization of rehabilitation research results. *Rehabilitation Education, 8*(4), 380–385.

Peytchev, A. (2009). Survey breakoff. *Public Opinion Quarterly, 73*(1), 74–97.

Peytchev, A., Couper, M. P., McCabe, S. E., & Crawford, S. D. (2006). Web survey design: Paging versus scrolling. *Public Opinion Quarterly, 70*(4), 596–607.

Schmitz, C., & Parsons, B. A. (1999). *Everything you wanted to know about logic models but were afraid to ask.* Boulder, CO: InSites. Retrieved from http://insites.org/insites_archive/documents/logmod.pdf

Seastrom, M. (2010a). *Basic concepts and definitions for privacy and confidentiality in student education records* (NCES 2011–601). Washington, DC: National Center for Education Statistics, Institute of Education Sciences, US Department of Education. Retrieved from http://nces.ed.gov/pubsearch/pubsinfo.asp?pubid=2011601/

Seastrom, M. (2010b). *Data stewardship: Managing personally identifiable information in electronic student education records* (NCES 2011–602). Washington, DC: National Center for Education Statistics, Institute of Education Sciences, US Department of Education. Retrieved from http://nces.ed.gov/pubsearch/pubsinfo.asp?pubid=2011602/

Seastrom, M. (2010c). *Statistical methods for protecting personally identifiable information in aggregate reporting* (NCES 2011–603). Washington, DC: National Center for Education Statistics, Institute of Education Sciences, US Department of Education. Retrieved from http://nces.ed.gov/pubsearch/pubsinfo.asp?pubid=2011603/

Small, P. (2012). Four differences between research and program evaluation [Web log post]. Minneapolis, MN: Authenticity Consulting, LLC. Retrieved from http://managementhelp.org/blogs/nonprofit-capacity-building/2012/01/08/four-differences-between-research-and-program-evaluation/

State Higher Education Executive Officers Association. (n.d.). *State postsecondary data systems.* Boulder, CO: SHEEOA. Retrieved from http://www.sheeo.org/sspds/default.htm

Taylor-Powell, E., & Henert, E. (2008) *Developing a logic model: Teaching and training guide.* Madison, WI: University of Wisconsin-Extension Cooperative Extension Program Development and Evaluation. Retrieved from www.uwex.edu/ces/pdande/evaluation/pdf/lmguidecomplete.pdf

University of North Carolina at Chapel Hill: The Writing Center. (n.d.). *Audience.* Chapel Hill, NC. Retrieved from http://writingcenter.unc.edu/handouts/audience/

US Department of Education. (n.d.). *Characteristics of statewide student data systems.* Washington, DC. Retrieved from http://nces.ed.gov/programs/slds/pdf/features_summary.pdf

US Department of Health and Human Services. (1979). *Belmont Report.* Washington, DC. Retrieved from http://www.hhs.gov/ohrp/humansubjects/guidance/belmont.html

What Works Clearinghouse. (2013). *Procedures and standards handbook, version 3.0.* Washington, DC: Institute of Education Sciences, US Department of Education. Retrieved from http://ies.ed.gov/ncee/wwc/documentsum.aspx?sid=19/

Wholey, J. S. (1987, Spring). Evaluability assessment: Developing program theory. *New Directions for Program Evaluation, 1987*(33), 77–92.

Additional Resources

Boyd, H. (n.d.). *Use comparison groups to strengthen your evaluation.* Madison, WI: University of Wisconsin System. Retrieved from http://www.uwex.edu/ces/pdande/resources/pdf/agenda.pdf

Coalition for Evidence Based Policy. (n.d.). *Identifying and implementing educational practices supported by rigorous evidence: A user-friendly guide.* Washington, DC: Institute of Education Sciences, US Department of Education. Retrieved from http://www2.ed.gov/rschstat/research/pubs/rigorousevid/rigorousevid.pdf

Conley, D. (2007). *Redefining college readiness.* Eugene, OR: Educational Policy Improvement Center. Retrieved from http://www.aypf.org/documents/RedefiningCollegeReadiness.pdf

Data Quality Campaign. (n.d.). *Alignment between the DQC's 10 essential elements and the America COMPETES Act's 12 elements.* Washington, DC: Author. Retrieved from http://www.dataqualitycampaign.org/files/851_America_COMPETES.pdf

Data Quality Campaign. (2012). *Data for action 2012: Focus on people to change data culture.* Washington, DC: Author. Retrieved from http://www.dataqualitycampaign.org/find-resources/data-for-action-2012/

Guo, S., Barth, R., & Gibbons, C. (2004). *Introduction to propensity score matching: A new device for program evaluation.* Retrieved from LearningAce website: http://www.learningace.com/doc/1719130/cb499a6328c93f4f3db09d8703842291/psm_sswr_2004

HealthKnowledge. (n.d.). *Introduction to study designs—Cohort studies.* Bucks, UK: Department of Health. Retrieved from http://www.healthknowledge.org.uk/e-learning/epidemiology/practitioners/introduction-study-design-cs

Khandker, S. R., Koolwal, G. B., & Samad, H. A. (2010). *Handbook on impact evaluation: quantitative methods and practices.* Washington, DC: The International Bank for Reconstruction and Development, The World Bank.

Miles, M. B., Huberman, A. M., & Saldaña, J. (2014). *Qualitative data analysis: A methods sourcebook* (3rd ed.). Thousand Oaks, CA: Sage.

National Center for Education Statistics. (2002). Section 5: Analysis of data: Production of estimates or projections. *Statistical Standards.* Washington, DC: National Center for Education Statistics, US Department of Education. Retrieved from http://nces.ed.gov/statprog/2002/std5_1.asp

National Center for Education Statistics. (2011). *Statistical methods for protecting personally identifiable information in aggregate reporting.* Washington, DC: National Center for Education Statistics, US Department of Education. Retrieved from http://nces.ed.gov/pubsearch/pubsinfo. asp?pubid=2011603

National Center for Education Statistics. (n.d.-a). Statewide Longitudinal Data Systems Grant Program. Washington, DC: National Center for Education Statistics, US Department of Education. Retrieved from http://nces.ed.gov/ Programs/SLDS/

National Center for Education Statistics. (n.d.-b). *Common education data standards.* Washington, DC: National Center for Education Statistics, US Department of Education. Retrieved from http://nces.ed.gov/programs/ ceds/

National Center for Education Statistics. (n.d.-c). *Privacy technical assistance center (PTAC).* Washington, DC: National Center for Education Statistics, US Department of Education. Retrieved from http://nces.ed.gov/programs/ ptac/Toolkit.aspx

Saldaña, J. (2013). *The coding manual for qualitative researchers* (2nd ed.). London: Sage.

Glossary

Activities approach model. A type of logic model that focuses on implementation and activities. This type of model is helpful for management and program monitoring (Kellogg Foundation, 2004).

Activities. One component of a logic model. Activities are the actions and interventions that are expected to produce the desired results.

Administrative records. Records maintained by the administrators of various programs.

Analysis of variance (ANOVA). A statistical test used to examine the differences in averages of more than two independent groups.

Application data. Information that describes how a student joined the program, including details about the student's eligibility and background.

Bias. Any tendency that prevents unprejudiced consideration of a question.

Categorical variable. A variable that can have a limited number of possible values.

Chi-square test. A statistical test of relationships between two categorical variables, showing whether they are independent from each other.

Choice. A dissemination method that actively helps users seek information and learn about options.

Codebook. A document containing details about each variable in a dataset.

Cohort. A group of individuals who have something in common, such as participating in a program during a specific year.

College ready. High school students who have the knowledge, skills, and characteristics that will allow them to succeed in postsecondary coursework without the need for remediation.

Control or comparison group. A group of students to whom the treatment group can be compared. A control group includes students who have similar characteristics but did not receive the service or participate in the program; a comparison group generally receives another treatment but not the one under investigation.

Content analysis. Methods for analyzing and summarizing text.

Content validity. A measure that has content validity captures all dimensions of a construct.

Correlation analysis. An analysis that focuses on the relationship between two variables. This type of analysis does not compare results from one group to another, but rather examines the strength of the relationship for all members of a single group.

Criterion validity. A measure that has criterion validity corresponds to an external measure in the expected way; for example, students who get good grades in algebra should do well on the end-of-course exam.

Data appending. The process of combining files that have different observations but the same variables.

Data breach. An unauthorized release of personally identifiable information.

Data dictionary. A document that describes each variable in a dataset.

Data merge. The process of combining datasets that have the same or related observations but different variables.

Demographic data. Descriptive information about course enrollment, attendance, family background, and other personal factors over which educators have no control.

Descriptive analysis. Analysis that describes the program, how it is working, and whether it is meeting its targets.

Dissemination. The transfer of knowledge with the expectation that it will be used.

Evidence of promise. Empirical evidence showing the link between at least one critical component of the program and at least one relevant outcome in the logic model.

Exchange. A dissemination method involving a two-way flow of information and interactions between people.

Experimental design. A set of steps involving randomly assigned treatment and control groups designed to determine or explain an observation by testing a hypothesis.

External variables. Variables that are not accounted for in the study design but may influence results.

Firewall. A network device that blocks certain kinds of network traffic, forming a barrier between a trusted and an untrusted network.

Formative evaluation. An evaluation that takes place during the intervention and focuses on the implementation process. Formative evaluations may provide information leading to immediate corrections to the services currently offered.

Hierarchical data. Data that have a tree-like, or nested, structure; for example, a dataset that includes records for school districts, schools within each district, and students within each school.

Hypothesis. An idea, or conjecture, that is structured as a statement to be proved or disproved with data.

Identifying data. Information (such as name, student identification number, Social Security number, birth date, and address) that identifies students and allows you to link program data with data from other sources.

Impact. One component of a logic model. The underlying intended result of the program.

Implementation. Use of new information with training, assistance, and support—the ultimate goal of most dissemination efforts that involve placing new programs in schools and enhancing classroom practices.

Inputs. One component of a logic model. Inputs are the resources available or needed to support initiation of the program plan.

Interval variable. An interval variable classifies observations by type and rank order and requires that differences between levels of the variable be equal (for example, temperature or intelligence as measured by IQ). The meaning for 0 is arbitrary; that is, 0 degrees does not mean that there is no temperature.

Logic model. A visual representation of how a program works, showing the theory and assumptions underlying the program, the sequence of activities, and how measurable outcomes are achieved. Logic models usually show inputs, activities, outputs, outcomes, and impact.

Longitudinal data. Information about the same individuals at multiple points in time.

Mean. Mathematical average.

Median. The central value in a group of numbers.

Mode. The number that occurs most frequently in a group. There may be more than one mode or no mode.

Multiple linear regression. A statistical method of controlling for multiple factors that may influence any given outcome.

Multiple measures. The idea (developed by Victoria Bernhardt; see Bernhardt, 1998) that researchers should consider four categories of data: demographic data, student performance data, perception data, and school process data (see separate definitions of these terms).

Multiple regression. An analytic strategy that allows simultaneous examination of multiple factors associated with an outcome.

Nominal variable. A variable that groups observations into discrete, mutually exclusive, and exhaustive categories, which are not ranked. This is also known as a categorical variable.

Ordinal variable. A variable that classifies observations by types, which are mutually exclusive and exhaustive, and are rank-ordered. That is, one category is regarded as better than another; for example, a letter grade of A is better than a letter grade of B.

Outcomes. One component of a logic model. Outcomes are changes that can be expected over time due to the increasing influence of outputs.

Outcomes approach model. A type of logic model that shows clear connections between the activities and the outcomes. These models are especially useful in designing program evaluations because they provide evaluators with measurable goals to assess.

Outputs. One component of a logic model. Outputs are immediate results that planners expect to be directly produced by the activities.

Perception data. Information about what various stakeholders (students, parents, and teachers) think of the school environment.